MW00328156

SHIFT
&
SHINE

SHIFT
&
SHINE

A MEMOIR

DEBORAH RICHARDS

Copyright © 2019
Library of Congress, Shift and Shine # TXu 2-140-551

DISCLAIMER This is a work of creative non-fiction, the events portrayed are to the best of Deborah Richards memory. Some names have been changed to protect the privacy of the people involved.

ISBN: 13:978-0578-52213-5

Cover and Interior design and formatting by

emtippettsbookdesigns.com

TABLE OF CONTENTS

I dedicate this book to my husband Jake, whom I love beyond oceans of time.

FOREWORD

By John Carl Stenzel

My name is John Carl Stenzel and I have worked in the field of addiction for the past 30 years. My dear friend Deborah Richards has told her story to the nth degree of honesty, health and self-care.

The story is told beautifully…...much of it I have known for years, since I was first introduced to her by a close and mutual friend. I have been and am still today honored to be part of her journey.

Deborah's book shows us determination, endurance, plus a simply beautiful, difficult and amazing life. For anyone dealing with addiction, death, and loss, its a must read.

To future readers of Shift and Shine, I encourage you to read this book, not for Deb, but for your own healing and "self-care." Through her wisdom and bravery, many who read this book can achieve a healthier way of living and a life of enjoyment in a much more meaningful manner.

Pay it forward to others.

PREFACE

My name is Deb and my husband described me as a cross between Katharine Hepburn and Faith Hill. (So amazingly sweet).

My friends describe me as a cross between Pippi Longstocking and Mary Poppins -- with a tablespoon of sugar. Ha! Maybe it's the nutty flavor.

This is my memoir, my story, my journey and my truth. To tell it, I need to tell you about my two daughters.

My daughters' unraveling journeys happened at a parallel time in history. Later, I would say that I was in denial while my therapist would say that I was innocent in my reactions, having had no experience with the oncoming journey.

I realize that perhaps it's best to start at the very beginning.

Even though I have never written a book before, I hear Dr. Wayne Dyer saying, "It does not matter if you have never painted, played a musical instrument, or written, simply begin. There will be something special that did not exist before. Don't die with your music inside of you."

I called the book, Shift and Shine, as I have learned to shift my thought and shine my light. I hope you might learn to do the same.

There is a line from the song Jake co-wrote that also applies here. He gave the world, "I love rock and roll. Put another dime in the jukebox, baby." I have indeed shown up despite all odds to put another dime in the jukebox!

I hope you won't judge me too harshly. I hope this book might help one human who has felt out of control and overwhelmed or who is dealing with violence, death and drugs.

As I am fond of saying, "Don't do what I did."

One note: Both my daughter and stepdaughter gave me permission to share their stories in the selfless hope that it will help others.

CHAPTER ONE

MY STORY

I grew up in the United Kingdom in one of those picturesque towns surrounded by green, grassy fields. My Mom and stepdad ran a village pub, and I have lovely memories of cold winter days and a fireplace with crackling and snapping wood greeting me on blustery days. My living room – which was basically the pub – was usually filled with fifty or sixty people including some strangers, but many old friends. Imagine always coming home to such a gathering.

I absolutely loved this. My Mom told me everyone has a story, and to be curious about their journey.

At the same time, my childhood was largely happy. As I grew into a teenager, I even had a role to play. If one of the waitresses called in sick, I was the one lifting a pint.

I had a deep love of the outdoors, into the fields to dream and wander I went. It wasn't surprising that I fell in love there – but not with a handsome boy. I loved the majestic horses that would roam on the back of the hill near where we lived, black and brown manes flying in the wind. Of course, I was like any other five-year-old girl with dreams of a saddle and a horse that belonged just to me. Somehow, I persuaded my mother and stepfather to buy me just a few riding lessons, but there would be no turning back. Ever.

Even at that age, I knew that horses somehow touched my soul. I couldn't know words like the source or the connection in those days. All I could do was reluctantly shimmy off my rented horse and spend as much time stroking his mane. I knew on a spiritual level that horses were pure and magnificent. Later, I would realize that horses have a God-given aura that's so pure and in the present moment that they reflect our own personal energy back to us.

It sounds so idyllic, but it was life. That meant there were bumps along the way.

My Mom became pregnant with me at age seventeen, which was a huge embarrassment for my grandparents who had adopted her from an orphanage when she was only nine. They had another biological daughter and longed to provide a sister to her. My future Mom, it turns out, was now giving them drama with her pregnancy. Even though I would never meet my biological father, my grandparents chose to accept me. They taught me that love is thicker than water and they loved me to pieces.

After I was born, Mom and I lived at my grandparent's house until I was six. I actually adored them and was quite sad when my Mom married. My stepfather was a very nice man – although extremely strict – which was a shock after my grandparents doting on me their granddaughter. Alas, we had to move on and create our own life.

It turns out I was quite enterprising when it came to achieving one of my biggest dreams.

At the ripe old age of twelve, I saved up fifteen pounds for a yearling horse – a twelve-month-old baby – who had been advertised for sale in the local paper. With an absolute clear and unrelenting will, I went about "encouraging" my grandparents to donate the other half of the money I needed.

Just 30 pounds and this dream could be mine, I thought.

I wrote out an official finance paper and delivered it to my parents, explaining how this would be achieved. It would be two pounds a month for his board at the local farmer's field and I would also need fifty pence a month for his hoof trimming. Of course, I would be able to afford all of this by getting a Saturday job. Much to my shock and joy, my parents actually deemed this outlandish plan as workable.

I ended up landing employment as the Saturday girl at the local sweets shop. I think I may have eaten more than I sold, but at least I fulfilled my part of this business arrangement – with a few milk chocolates as my own personal bonus.

Finally, it was the big day and a young, very scared baby brown horse with a star on his beautiful forehead was delivered to the farmer's field. The only trouble was I couldn't catch him for the first six months because he wouldn't come near me! I chose not to worry, but simply sat in the field and talked to him until he was curious enough to wander close. But not too close because we were in the beginning stages.

I couldn't know it was a metaphor for life: One step closer. One step back. One step closer …… hold your breath… another step.

Then he came even closer until I was able to brush him and love on him. The business of riding was next. At first, I leaned gently on his back and then put a bit of weight on, ready to retract if the pressure was too much. He could handle it, and I could let out the air I had been holding. How I longed for this beautiful boy to fly me across that grassy green.

"Breathe and keep a soft bottom," I reminded myself.

And we were off!

In that moment, I knew joy.

You're probably wondering what I named my precious boy. I called him Saladin after the famous Turkish warrior who had interacted with Richard the Lionheart, Richard I of England. We were studying that period in history at school. Saladin displayed all the magnificent qualities of innate intelligence and ultimate fairness. I called him "Lad" as a nickname and on so many days, Lad and I would just walk side-by-side through the field.

On some of those dreamy days, I'd skip school just to breathe in my horse's pungent scent as I poured out everything in my teenage heart. What was there to tell? What wasn't there to tell? Lad could be trusted with anything. That's what young girls do with horses. We talk and they listen.

It was so simple. So pure. So beautiful.

My Lad wouldn't be the last horse who would provide this service. You could call it therapy, but I prefer to think of it as something divine.

Of course, life had a funny way of intervening on all this bliss as time moved me along. My parents decided to transfer me to a private school for my high school years. It was called St. Hilda's School for Young Ladies and I'm not sure if even St. Hilda herself succeeded on the latter part of that statement. This school was designed to craft encouraging futures. The truth was, I loved it there because it felt safe and they encouraged little bookworms like me.

It was also very, very British. There was even a British dress code and when it was warm outside, I wore a summer straw boater. The cold brought out my winter velour hat. You didn't dare wander off school property without your hats on and somehow this crept into my psyche. Even now my friends tease me about my love of hats, no matter the circumstance. St. Hilda would be so proud.

I do not, however, wear an apron at lunch as we did during those high school days.

At home, my parents were divided when describing the kind of young woman that I was blossoming into in front of their eyes. My father would say I was precocious and way too spirited, while my mother said I was book smart but had no common sense. I prefer to say I was gullible and very trusting. All these traits somehow graduated with me after high school – especially the trusting trait.

I was 18 and a newly minted adult. After being around all those girls, I was quite ready for the world – including meeting boys.

Even more exciting than meeting a young man was my first dream of working as a stage actress. This didn't thrill my parents who suggested I go to college first and get some real skills under my belt. "What about typing?" my Mom asked in a hopeful voice. "Then you might actually be able to feed yourself."

Mom reminded me that when actors said they were "resting," it was just another term for unemployed. I was sure the world could not wait to see my thespian skills. Yet, I dutifully started college, fretting that I would be too old to act if I had to wait four whole years.

With the same willpower I put into getting Lad, I researched how to get a scholarship to acting schools. In the end, I auditioned for three of the top schools and was turned down by only one. I was ecstatic, but still needed the money to pay the tuition and housing. There were a few unexpected twists along the way. I had to audition in front of a group for scholarships and was asked if I would cut all my hair off for the play, Joan of Arc.

What a silly question.

Of course I would.

I was dedicated, determined and young. That's a dangerous combination.

To my parents' astonishment (and my joy), a letter arrived in the mail telling me that I had received a full scholarship to drama school! The thespian world would no longer have to wait because I was dropping out of college to follow my dream.

From the start, I discovered that acting school would be a far different experience. Start with the fact that people from all ages attended and the core curriculum was a bit odd. I was told that I'd find my inner pirate by learning how to fence, which was so Pirates of the Caribbean of them. I wasn't convinced that there would be throngs of swashbuckling roles in my future, but took my fencing lessons seriously. The only issue was my own novice status with weapons befitting someone with an eye patch and bird on her shoulder. I had a rather blonde moment when I asked the instructor, "Should I remove the rubber tip at the end of the sword?"

Slice and dice would take on a whole new meaning.

Quite happily, I was busy emoting and embraced the fact that the school studied the Stanislavski Method, which meant you had to immerse body, mind and soul to get totally (and I mean with every ounce of your being) into a character. Case in point: The professors thought it was wonderful when a second-year student was so "in character" that he jumped out of a third story window!

In the end, he wasn't dead, which was a relief. (Although if it was a death scene, I had to wonder if he was fully committed to his character!) Bruised and bloodied, he received an "A" for his efforts. Meanwhile, I was playing Tatiana in Shakespeare's A Midsummer

Night's Dream. Sadly, I didn't get a particularly good review.

My teacher finally commented, "More twigs and flowers seem to be appearing on your head each day."

Really? What did they expect on a student's rather abysmal income? I couldn't exactly afford real costumes.

One of the joys of acting school was the interesting upcoming artists that I met and considered my friends. On the weekends, we'd go to the local hotel on a Sunday night and dance the night away at the disco. Oh, how I loved to dance! One night, a stranger approached and when I looked up, I saw a manly, handsome face smiling down at me. His eyes had that sparkle and I knew in those early moments that he could charm the birds from the tree. He certainly charmed me as I danced a very slow number with him. He was muscular and commanding while I was young and inexperienced. I was 19; he was 34. In other words, he was every parent's nightmare of a potential son-in-law and every young woman's idea of living on the edge.

I was smitten and as I got to know Charlie better, I found him worldly. He seemed to know everything about everything. Even when I was given bouts of thinking maybe I knew something, he would overrule me. One of his thoughts was that perhaps I should drop out of drama school and so I did. I was in love.

Who needed Shakespeare? I would soon be living my own very real-life drama and there was no apparent window to jump out of in order to save myself. When I was 21, we married despite my parents' objections and soon I gave birth in pretty excruciating pain to a beautiful baby daughter I named Haley. Oh, how I fell in love with her. It's so true that you never experience the love for a spouse that you have for your child. I knew, as God is my witness, I would protect her from anyone.

From everything.

Little did I know she would need protecting so early in her life.

As time progressed, it turned out that Charlie could not only charm those birds from the sky, but I learned that he liked to crush them under his big, black boots without blinking.

His background had always been a bit blurry and he provided an unsettling clarity after we tied the knot. It turns out that Charlie had been to prison a few times for armed robbery. As infatuation faded, I realized that I was just plain scared of him. It didn't help that he moved us to a remote farmhouse, hours away from my parents and friends. All alone with the baby during the day while Charlie worked running his new nightclub, I would reflect on my earlier, much happier days when family didn't mean fear.

There were times when I would scold myself.

Hadn't I just jumped the line of life? Wasn't I lucky to be 22, living on my own farm and the proud mother of a gorgeous baby daughter? There were days when I could actually convince myself that I was leading a dream life. The truth was a sobering wake-up call. I was stunningly lonely most of the time and afraid the rest of the time. That's a toxic mix.

Little Haley and I muddled through those long days in isolation together. My ties to the outside world were almost non-existent. The phone Charlie had installed needed coins to make it work and he would only leave me with enough money to make emergency calls. "I don't need you wasting money talking to your friends and family," he barked.

I felt helpless and frightened.

It's true that he left me a car – the one with only one seat. So I would bundle up my darling daughter on the floor beside me and try to make it down the dirt road, which was over a mile in distance. In the winter, we were virtually shut-ins because the road was just about impassable. I needed a four-wheel, all-terrain vehicle to make it out of there.

One day, the nice farmer next door saw me struggling in the middle of a weather-ravaged field and pulled my car out of thick mud.

It was a feat that he repeated more times than I care to remember.

When Charlie returned, he wasn't always alone, and that was heart stopping. He'd roll up in his older, maroon Rolls Royce (Haley would call it "Daddy's Roller") with three friends – bouncer/thug-types – riding shotgun. It was his version of a posse – or his own private Mafia. The men were large and mean and I was scared of all of them, including the one who slept next to me.

It was a warm spring morning when Haley proved that my fears weren't unfounded. Glancing outside my kitchen window, my face went pale when I saw ten police cars roaring up to the house, sirens blaring. Officers swarmed out with guns drawn. The British police are not supposed to carry guns, I thought, holding my daughter tightly as the absurdity of what was unfolding played out in front of my eyes. I was in a dream…no, a fricking nightmare.

"This is not happening," I whispered. "Not…happening."

But, it was.

In the end, I found out that a policeman had noticed two sawed off shotguns near our fireplace and had obtained a search warrant to find out exactly what was going on in Charlie's world, which unfortunately was also my world.

The bitter taste of bile filled my throat and my stomach flipped. By now, Haley was four and I thanked God that she couldn't understand what was happening in the horror film that was our lives. I had to play it off as some crazy adventure with "those nice policemen visiting us to say hello."

I couldn't tell her that her father was a known criminal.

As Charlie felt the pressure of additional eyes on him, he became increasingly irritated and abusive. Did I have the food cans lined up in alphabetical order? I watched the Julia Roberts movie *Sleeping with the Enemy* some years later and thought, Wow, someone has written my life story. If the cans were not correctly lined up alphabetically, he flew into a rage. Was his shirt ironed perfectly? If not, he would scream at me. One day, he was consumed with such white-hot anger that he ripped off his shirt, popping all the buttons like the Incredible Hulk. Apparently, I had not ironed his collar correctly and his naked eye found exactly one wrinkle.

One.

"I will never iron again," I vowed to myself.

A mountain of a man, Charlie didn't hesitate getting physical to express his displeasure. An explosive fight one night resulted in me taking a header down the long, wooden staircase. I landed on the hard floor with the wind knocked out of me.

I was six months pregnant with Haley.

He would go from berating to punching me. One swift smack with his knuckle to my mouth split my lip and face open. I have the scar to this day and will never erase the memory of blood filling my mouth and running down my face. I can still hear the crunching of my teeth and feel the desperate shaking of my body.

Oh, what had I done by marrying this monster?

One day for no particular reason that I knew, he came home from his club and destroyed all of our furniture with his bare hands. No one saw the wake of his temper except for his helpless wife and baby daughter.

He kept yellow Jiff bottles that in the UK are normally filled with lemon juice. I was shocked to realize that he had replaced the liquid with battery acid, which he menacingly threatened to throw in my face. "Don't you even dare dream of leaving me, Deb!" he'd rant. "No one will ever look at you again once the acid eats your skin." Even as I write this now, my blood runs cold and my heart races. I imagine that young, naïve young woman who was drowning, inch by inch, gulp by gulp.

Was I just annoying to him?

Or maybe, by nature, he was just a cold, bullying torturer!

I knew I had to leave him, and somewhere deep inside, there was a last ounce of courage. It was never about the things we had together, although I knew he would argue over the last knife and fork. He thrived on contention, as many bullies do. All I wanted to do was physically leave with my daughter and run as far as possible. Yet, I didn't even have suitcases to pack our clothing. I did, however, have some rather large black trash bags.

Who said that necessity was the mother of invention? Or perhaps mothers in need will do anything – invent anything or use anything – to escape with their children.

Leaving wasn't a quick process. By the time I ran, I had a four-year-old with me and I had to keep her life as normal as possible. That meant bolting from the farm under the strict cover of secrecy and then staying on various sofas while dealing with the fact that I didn't even have enough money with me to get through a week, let alone start a new life. We had physically left Charlie but were plunged into another kind of nightmare where we were equally vulnerable. The silver lining was my darling daughter who was such a happy, joyful little girl and loved our "adventure" where we'd "hide" with my compassionate, amazing friends who provided shelter.

Emotionally, it was hard for Haley because she was never subjected personally to Charlie's abuse. He loved her unconditionally; thank God he had never laid a hand on her. Yet, she was front and center witnessing the abuse of her Mom, which must have been hard.

When she asked for Dad, I told her that he needed to be alone right now. That's why we were going to live in a room I rented in a house. Luckily, my roommate at the house was the same age as me and our friendship grew. Lindsay didn't mind living with a single Mom – although she didn't like the fact that eventually Charlie found us and visited when the whim struck him.

He would just appear, unannounced with his "gang," and demand to take Haley for the afternoon.

"Do I have to go? I don't want you to be alone Mommy ?" my little girl would ask in a shaking voice and it shattered my heart.

For hours I'd sit alone in our rental room praying and then pacing – wondering if he would ever return her— knowing that his ultimate revenge against me would be keeping our child. The minutes were so slow and those days never seemed to end. Eventually, I'd hear the front door open and her little shoes run across the tile. The breath I had been holding would come out in ragged relief. Another day of Charlie's wrath was over. We had somehow made it through.

"I'll never pay you a penny of support. I won't even pay child support," he threatened. "I'll even deny I'm her father." How much lower could he sink? This was in the days before paternity testing. What Charlie didn't know is that I would have loved it if he weren't her natural father.

Meanwhile, my choices were grim. I could move again, but he would certainly find us. Was no place safe from a man this ferocious? As someone who likes to avoid conflict because it makes me feel physically sick, I felt trapped like a scared mouse in a box. I had been raised to apologize if *you* stood on *my* foot. Talk about stuffing your feelings down.

I'm not sure how the new plan formed, but it was an inspired one.

"What if we moved to America?" Lindsay asked one night when we were talking into the wee hours. "Haley could have a new start there and experience a happy childhood without this man and his thugs in her life. She could have a chance at the American dream.

And Deb, you could pursue your acting again".

In that instant I knew I could find the strength to flee for my daughter.

I vowed she would not suffer for the dreadful choices I made so far in my own young life.

We would move to America. It had been decided.

I was determined. I was clueless. I figured that maybe – just maybe – those two variables when put together could turn into a good thing.

I started the process by studying America and learned that there was no real class system there, which was something I disliked about the United Kingdom. "In America, Haley, you can grow up to be anything you want," I promised her. I didn't add these words, "Regardless of who your father was…or was not."

As I have never met my father, that seemed sort of liberating.

America promised to be a land of forward thinkers. If you wanted to change something that had always been done a certain way, then America was the place to do it. The British folk would say, "Why?" Americans would say, "Why not?" The class system I grew up with would melt away… there would be no stopping us!

As usual, money stood between the dream and the reality. So I started to save, selling some of my few belongings and skimping on everything.

I told my Mom that in America "the sun is shining, and I can already speak the language."

Fate intervened when Charlie did God-only-knows-what and landed in jail again. That was a gift wrapped in a shining red bow.

We flew the coop, which is a nice way of saying it. The truth was I kidnapped my own daughter and felt absolutely no remorse about it because there was no other choice.

The year was 1997.

What an odd sight we must have been at American customs in Los Angeles. I looked nervous and was flanked by my now six-year-old daughter, Lindsay (who had decided to relocate with us) and her German Shepherd, Cain. Apparently, there were no quarantine laws in the U.S. in those days so, bringing Cain with us was much easier than what one might imagine. I was so grateful because I couldn't have made the move without Lindsay.

I had two suitcases with me. (I left the trash bags back in England!) One of those cases was filled to the brim with about thirty My Little Pony toys. The other case contained all our clothes – the pieces I didn't sell to pay for the trip. I was sure that customs would spring open my case, all these plastic horses would fall out and they would find us utterly suspicious. They would then know that I could not have possibly come for the standard two-week visit. There were just too many ponies to believe that one!

In the end, customs could not have cared less and I surmised that they had seen far stranger things in bags that were searched. Meanwhile, Lindsay knew an American she had met in the UK and had arranged for the young man, an actor, to pick us up at LAX airport.

"How hard can our new life be?" I whispered to myself.

Those were famous last words.

The actor didn't show up for hours and poor Haley got cranky and started to cry as we waited in the airport. "I want to go home!" she wailed.

When he finally collected us, he took us directly to the local racetrack and then borrowed money from the both of us to make his bets. This was not exactly the start I had expected. Our Los Angeles dream next moved to a seedy Motel 6 where we would stay after we smuggled Cain the dog in through a window. I was so glad the dog was with us because he made me feel secure. Plus, Haley loved him. He was a live, huge and cuddly security system with fur.

Haley was delighted when we had breakfast at the IHOP next door. "Mom" she whispered – her eyes round as saucers – "They eat dessert for breakfast here!" A huge stack of pancakes and whipped cream disappeared before my eyes.

The next day, Lindsay called her other American friend who drove us around to look at apartments. We had about $2,000 between us, but somehow, we found a place to share on Fountain Avenue – which wasn't exactly a safe location. On the plus side, it had two bedrooms and we were thrilled. "We're camping, Haley," I told my little girl as I made our beds, using clothes as sheets. Then I lined up all those little ponies.

I was liberated.

We were free.

And I was very, very happy as I mentally left frantic survival mode and willed myself back to present moment living.

CHAPTER TWO

COMING TO AMERICA

Moving to America was like transporting my life into a movie – but it wasn't as simple as *mother and daughter walk off into that brilliant California sunset.* There was still the proverbial bad guy lurking somewhere: my ex. Although I felt confident that he would have to exert a great deal of intention to find us, I wouldn't allow myself to be consumed with that worry, vowing to put him out of my mind once and for all. There was too much life to live in our new home.

Oh, the land of opportunity! Middle of the night fear sessions could wait because I wanted to simply breathe and enjoy my new life. The streets may not have been paved with gold outside our apartment, but the sunshine was free and life was just better. I delighted in the fact that Haley was settling well into her new home. She was happy and laughing, as I had wanted. Her favorite place on the planet became the Hollywood dog park on Laurel Canyon where we took Cain on those hot summer days.

Sitting under the sprinklers that were there to water the grass (and us), we'd have picnics. Haley would entertain herself – and everyone else – by walking all the different breeds of dogs, taking each one for a turn around the park. The owners were enchanted by Haley's English accent and her gentleness with their beloved animals. She was also such a beautiful child with her tawny brown hair and huge brown eyes, the color so dark you could not tell where the pupils ended, and the color began.

Meanwhile, Lindsay, Haley and I (and the dog) were inseparable as we hitchhiked around Los Angeles – which I know sounds alarming. Our flaw in those days (or perhaps our anchor) was our optimism. I reasoned, "What lunatic would pick up this strange little group with the extremely large dog?" The truth was our guardian angel must have been working overtime throughout those years.

As the days passed, the memories of abuse began to fade and feel quite far away. Once again, the nights were peaceful, and I'd watch my Haley sleeping as my heart melted at the sight of her unlined angel face at rest. *Oh, how we love our children.*

How was I to know then that my choices inextricably affected how I would interact with my daughter in the future?

Daddy became a ghost. We never mentioned her bio-father, as I now thought of him. I believe Haley understood there were shadows we didn't want to walk in any longer. On a more basic level, she instinctually knew that any mention of her bio-father would certainly make me nervous and unhappy. She didn't want to see her Mom like that ever again. To be fair to her, I refrained from saying anything bad about Charlie – although I preferred to think of him as gone. Very gone.

The strange thing was that occasionally I would honestly believe I caught a glimpse of his malicious face in the crowd. A blink later, I'd luckily realize that it wasn't him. It took a moment, however, for my ragged breathing to return to normal.

Over time, Lindsay and I made many new friends that we mostly met at that dog park. One of them invited us to a wrap party for some new movie, which sounded so glamorous and very Hollywood. I'll never forget wandering around a lavish mansion feeling quite far removed from my previous life. The people were so beautiful, and the vibe was exciting. Dating was the last thing on my mind, but I still found it amusing when a very handsome man began to follow me around. *Why? Why has he chosen me?* I began to wonder.

His name was Jake.

He had dark brown eyes, the most succulent lips and a mane of dark flowing hair. He was extremely fit.

Eventually, we traded the usual information while I learned that he was an award-winning music writer who co-wrote the classic rock song, "I Love Rock and Roll." He was from New York, a super over-achiever, gifted and intelligent. It was clear that he did not suffer fools. He told me he was separated from his wife.

I deemed him worthy of being a white knight in shining armor. In fact, his story was amazing. His parents survived the Holocaust and most of his extended aunts and uncles died there, which was just horrific. After the war, his parents fled to Israel where Jake was born, in Haifa. They emigrated to the United States when Jake was six. His father worked as a butcher, which made it easier, but it was still a tough transition. They had to learn to speak English in order to survive in this new country. Jake would laughingly say he was dragged to the wrong part of the Bronx when he really belonged in sunny Los Angeles.

This led to him playing guitar for ten hours a day or until his fingers bled. He told me tales of running away when he was 13 and taking the train to New York, and Café Wa, a local music spot. Where upon arrival he would sleep in people's bathtubs. Anything to achieve his dream of being in a band.

With absolute determination, with his bandmate and friend, they eventually took a journey to the UK to set about getting a deal.

They met with Mickie Most, a famous UK producer and played him, "I Love Rock and Roll," a tune Mickie said was – at best – a side B cut. Jake and his friend wouldn't be deterred. They formed the group, The Arrows, and Mickie helped with getting them a variety TV show gig.

It wasn't long before the big time came knocking and he was having the time of his life!

Joan Jett recorded "I Love Rock and Roll" and – as they say – the rest is history. He went on to write amazing songs for *Rocky IV* and *Top Gun*, too.

But back to the start of this love story….

Later, Jake would say that just seeing me across that crowded room was love at first sight. I would laugh at his words and say, "More like lust at first sight!"

"No, love," he said firmly, insisting that the fabled thunderbolt struck him at first glance.

I began to date Jake while he worked out the particulars of a messy divorce with a child, a little boy he clearly adored. As time progressed, I began to subscribe to the thunderbolt theory, too. I was feeling those thunderbolts each time I heard his voice. My hopes were high as my heart insisted that he could very well be my true soulmate.

Another sunny California day and Jake was coming over. My heart began to sing until I saw the look on his face. Pained is an understatement. "Deb, I am so sorry, but I can't see you anymore. I need to give my marriage another chance for the sake of my son."

I was stomach punched, but once I took a deep breath – or a few – I realized that I was also in awe of this man's integrity and love for his child. As someone who relocated to a new country for her child, I could put my feelings aside and found admiration for his choice.

Once again, I had to pick up the pieces. Mothers know that you wake up, make breakfast and go through the motions of a day even when your heart is splattered all over that nice floor you just washed.

Five years in America seemed to pass in a blur and I had moved to Santa Barbara to take a job I absolutely loved. I became the PR salesperson for a title company, and I couldn't believe that we were able to live in this paradise of beaches and sun while I got paid to take lovely humans to lunch and dinner.

I was absolutely happy in my own skin.

One day, a platonic friend named Kenny called and said, "Deb, you'll never guess who had a baby today?" For some reason, I could absolutely guess.

"Jake," I said, knowing that I hit the nail on the head.

He confirmed that it was a girl and by now I could honestly say, "I wish them the best. I hope it all goes well for them."

When we hung up the phone, I tried to imagine the face of this precious angel girl baby. This wasn't time to be sad for myself. It was time to celebrate the first day of her life on this planet. Her name would be Natasha.

Some 18 months passed and Kenny called with additional news. "You'll never guess who is separated again and dating everyone," he confided.

"Jake."

Of course, I could guess.

"He asked me to call you," Kenny said. "He wanted to see if he could bring his son up to stay at your place and go to the Santa Barbara zoo?"

One word. It would decide my fate over the next decades.

"Sure," I said in a hesitant voice as my heart skipped a small beat.

I had wonderful girlfriends and told a few of them that this man Jake was coming to stay in my spare room for the weekend. "If any of you like him then go for it!" I said. "I've been there, done that and got the T-shirt!"

It wasn't long before there was a knock on the door.

It turned out that Jake hadn't changed one bit and the little boy was precious and easy to be around. I was wary around his father as I willed my heart to stay in deep freeze mode. It was a platonic and friendly visit that ended with no future promises. Later, he did call to say thank you. And then he called again. And again.

Deep freeze was melting.

As the holidays drew near, he asked me what I was doing for New Year's Eve. "Jackie, my roommate and I are having a party here at the house," I responded.

"Will it be any good?" Jake asked.

I remember my brain trying to find an answer that would satisfy both of us. "Well, I really can't speak to that," I responded, adding, "I bring my own fun with me wherever I go."

He turned up at that New Year's Eve party looking so handsome that my mouth dropped open. But I was speechless for other reasons. On each arm, he had a stunning young Asian woman. In fact, all the men at the party gravitated toward this little group because they wanted whatever catnip Jake was using. I smiled and said to my friend Jackie, "How very Jake-ish of him."

All I can say is that the party rocked. At one point, Jackie pulled me to the side and said, "Deb, I really think the house is going to fall off the stilts, down the hill and into the ocean." The idea of a floating party seemed quite novel to me! After reassuring her that we would be fine (with my fingers crossed behind my back), I began to ignore Jake and enjoy myself. Did I mention that I had also brought a date to the party? He was a very gregarious man who was an appreciator of women far and wide.

All night long I could feel Jake staring at us, and at one point he emerged from nowhere and pulled me onto the dance floor. I looked up into his beautiful face allowing myself to dream that it was actually *our time*. Alas, it was just a dream because he left with his two female guests. Later, I found myself quite alone because my own date had hightailed it out of there in a huff.

All this push-pull was merely our opening act. Jake and I kept gravitating towards each other, and eventually all the rest fell by the wayside.

He called and invited me to attend the Comedy Awards in Los Angeles and I chatted with Jackie my amazing beautiful British bright friend before committing to this date. "It's too far to drive. Who will look after Haley and Bongo, our dog?" I queried as I tried to convince myself to stay home.

Ever loving Jackie said she would look after everything. "Just go, Deb," she said. Jackie had grown up in the same area as me, but we did not start our friendship until I moved to America. Jackie is one of those selfless humans everyone wishes they had as a friend.

I had the most amazing evening, and the highlight of that visit was being introduced to his 18-month old daughter, Natasha. Oh my God, I fell in love all over again when I gazed at this breathing, blonde-haired, blue-eyed baby doll.

She was perfection.

Months passed and the distance between my home in Santa Barbara and Los Angeles was difficult. So, eventually we moved in together with all the kidlets and it felt warm, cozy and fun. His home in those days was located in the Hollywood Hills, which – although really beautiful – was also a hectic place of young actors, musicians and others vying for their spot in show business. When I drove down the hill to Hollywood Boulevard, I was shocked to see that the local grocery store had an armed guard outside. It was just so different from gentle Santa Barbara with Butterfly Beach and amber sunsets. (Jake said he expected me to make a bolt back to SB, as I was in such culture shock.)

The upside was that Jake's house had a really pretty pool with flowers that grew almost into the water. I'd walk about there and swear that I was in Hawaii. Our three kids lived in that pool and soon their skin turned into a mottled texture that only skin left in water does. I was convinced they had no nerve endings!

Many of their friends would hang out at our home, which made me so happy because it was always filled with shrieks of laughter and a good kind of chaos. It was such a happy time that I fully lived in. Now, I treasure those joyous moments.

Jake was the one who brought up making our blended family legal.

Or maybe I said the words, "I need a Green Card."

Smiling, Jake would say: "Deb, that's the most romantic thing I've ever heard."

He would also tease me that he needed to catch me between marriages (there was a 10-month one in the middle that doesn't seem worth mentioning), and later he would laugh and say that I did marry him for that Green Card. That caused us many chuckles over the years.

The truth was Jake would constantly tell me that he "loved me beyond oceans of time." He told me he loved me in past lives and would always find me in future ones.

I would borrow Winnie the Pooh's line and say, "If you live to be a hundred, I want to live to be a hundred minus one day, so I never have to live without you."

I meant that with all my being.

He was such a romantic man. Once when I was away on business in Arizona, I returned tired and cranky from delayed flights. Jake had made plans for the kidlets to be looked after by friends. I walked in the door to find hundreds of rose petals scattered all over the house, candles lit, and beautiful Spanish acoustic music wafting through the air.

"Sit down, baby" he said," I wrote a song for you".

He pulled out his guitar and began to gently sing a song he had written just for me called, "Dancing on Stars." The words went like this:

SHIFT & SHINE

My love is dancing on stars
Caped in moonbeams
With comets in her hair
She crosses the universe
With a step and a sigh
I see all that there is
Whenever she is near
She is dancing on stars
Time bows down to my lady aglow
She is both unborn and undead
A great mystery lost through eternity
Now found in my heart and in my head
My love is dancing on stars
Caped in moonbeams
With comets in her hair
She crosses the universe with a step and a sigh
I see all that there is
Whenever she is near
My love is dancing on stars
Her lips as wet as the sea
With skin as white as a dove
No greater beauty has been seen
No feeling greater than my love
She crosses the universe
With a step and a sigh
I see all that there is
Whenever she is near
My love is dancing on stars
Caped in moonbeams
With comets in her hair
She will forever be dancing on stars. By Jake for Deb xxx

It was one of the most beautiful love songs I ever heard. How blessed I was to be loved by this man who gave me his feelings in full.

These were lean times for him, but we scraped together $500 to purchase my beautiful blue topaz ring, which is still one of my treasures because it was my engagement ring. I'd glance down at my finger and swear I was wearing a piece of the sky or the ocean on my finger.

I adored Jake and he adored me right back. I was his fairy on top of the Christmas tree, and he was always my rock who would gently nudge me off the dance floor to go home.

"Just five more minutes?" I'd ask.

"No baby, time to go" he would say.

Deep down, I'd feel so fortunate that this was one of our bigger "issues" as a couple. The truth is without Jake as my anchor, I would have stayed out there way too long.

Our couple life was as solid as rock. It was just a matter now of truly blending as a family.

I came home from a three-week stay in the hospital to find an amazing gift from him, which was a trip to Jamaica. It was one of the most romantic experiences of my life. Each day, we stared out at crystal clear ocean, laughing as we sipped umbrella drinks and floated on that calm water. We'd make exquisite love every afternoon while the thunderstorms rolled in. It was just the two of us.

So content.

So very much in love.

CHAPTER THREE

LOVE IS THICKER THAN WATER

I married Jake when Haley was 12, which is a difficult age for any child – especially a girl who was entering her hormonal time of life and was quite used to having her Mommy all to herself. Despite a few bumps, life remained a dream. We moved into a house in Pacific Palisades which was a cute, modest, one-story home that we filled with love. Luckily, there was a pool for the kidlets.

We spent so much time outdoors with music blasting as we all danced around the pool. There was no need to go anywhere else but where we were.

I relished being a stepmom to my new ready-made family and pictured our life like one of those charming Norman Rockwell paintings. My goal was for everything to be fair for everyone, and thus prove that love is thicker than water – not blood. I knew that you could never have too many people who love you, and I still believe that to this day. My grandparents had shown me this and I had experienced this firsthand being a stepchild.

Jake and I would bring the love to this mix.

Of course, things weren't perfect. Jake returned to AA, which he started while we were dating. His demons were being conquered and I saw him act as a wonderful father to his children who mostly lived with us while their mother, a singer, was on tour. His children were the operative words here. Deep down, I felt as if Haley still only had me, and I remained her single Mom in my brain. I knew I could do it all: Superwoman, Provider, Fixer, Enabler and Holder of the Credit Card Mom. With hindsight being twenty-twenty, I think one of me – with the damage I enabled – was more than enough.

It made me sad that Haley remained her own island. I used to think how great it would have been if she could have gone with her stepbrother and stepsister to Exey's house (the name I fondly called his ex) because it sounded like so much fun. Jake's son Jason would come back with stories about how they went out to lunch and to the latest movie. There were presents and swim sessions. When she came home after being on tour, it was almost like your fairy Godmother swooping back into town to have big huge unending fun.

As the years passed, it broke my heart when Jake told Haley to stay in her room when her stepsiblings left. I remember Haley eating dinner in her room by herself while Jake asked for some one-on-one time alone with his wife. As I write these words, I look back at myself with such disgust. How could I have allowed it? But I did because I craved a happy marriage and a family and thought that there was no sacrifice too great to keep it intact. The Brady Bunch lives on! For some reason, it made my husband feel awkward to have my daughter around without his biological kids. No, she can't come to the movies with us. It's our alone time.

The line was drawn. My tightrope was strung.

When all the kids were there, we were a family unit. If not, I was a wife.

As with most families, our lives fell into a mold that set quickly.

I began to fall into a pattern of figuring out ways to keep Jake and Haley separated from each other while giving both an equal amount of attention.

I loved them both more than life and I wasn't going through a divorce. I would never ever leave Jake because I loved him with my entire heart. I was absolutely convinced that somehow, I could provide Haley with a happy family unit. I reasoned that her new siblings were wonderful additions to her life, and there were countless happy family times with all the children present.

One warm summer night found Haley, Jason and little Natasha running through the grass of our new home in Malibu simply screaming with joy as they played Capture the Flag. All the neighborhood kids joined in... I grasped these moments, wishing I never had to let go. There was so much good here. This was my justification for deciding the choices I made were the right ones.

Another night, I found Haley in Natasha's bedroom on the floor playing stuffed animals with the toddler. This filled my heart.

There was love of the abundant variety.

My stepdaughter Natasha enjoyed a journey that was far different from my biological daughter's path in life. This little girl had four parents who clearly adored her – Exey, Jake, her stepfather and me. I was dubbed DebMama. I was shocked when later she informed me, "It was two parents too many."

I chuckled, and I understood. She had double the amount of people deciding her future.

Exey was away on tour for months at a time, so I got to have this beautiful little person pretty much full time. In some ways, I'll always think that I was a better mother to her than to Haley whom

I gave birth to when I was too young to know better. Haley and I grew up together and struggled. Natasha and I had the time and my wisdom to enjoy our early moments together. As she grew, she was an adventurous child who loved to go with me to buy flowers or would join me in our own garden and plant new seeds. This was the type of child who would stop to really look at a sunset. Jake loved the fact that I was so thrilled with her and I'd tell him, "Even though she's not of my blood, she's of my essence."

It was like being given a beautiful doll, and I'll admit that it was hard to give her back when the Exey came back into town. We fell into an easy routine that sometimes got disrupted when she returned and later would have to re-learn our home life. Again, this was tough for Haley who had to adjust to the comings and goings of her siblings.

As time moved on, I was also overwhelmed by family life and working full time.

When Jake and I first got together, I needed to find a job. I saw an ad that said a real estate background would be helpful. I went for the interview, passed the first round and then flew to Oklahoma for the second round of interviews. I got the job, Hallelujah! I was to oversee sales for the western United States for nationwide ALTA Land Surveys. For the first six months, I could not get arrested! I had absolutely no idea of what I was doing – none – and could not find anyone who wanted this service. I was sure I would be fired.

Jake had an amazing work ethic, and he inspired me every single day to stay with it and keep trying. Eureka! One day, a light bulb went off and I understood. I nailed my client base and went on to be a rock star of that industry, if I do say so myself. I also thoroughly enjoyed it.

The home front was also impossibly busy. When two people suddenly turn into five, there is just so much more in terms of laundry, cooking, scheduling and beyond. But I was Uber Mom extraordinaire. I'd plan a business trip to Atlanta to see clients and then get a call from Exey four days before leaving saying, "Sorry, but

I'm out of town next week."

I was constantly rearranging to keep the peace. But in her defense, she really did not have control over her schedule. When she booked a gig, she had to go. Meanwhile, I was that helicopter Mom who was always there, always dependable and always saving the day. Sure, I'd rearrange my schedule. I knew what everybody should be doing at all times and made sure that the wheels kept spinning. The key was for the kids to excel and have fun.

I was living on adrenalin. My motto was: The more I do, the more I can do. I needed a 48-hour day to get it all done, but I still managed to squeeze it all into a tight 24 hours. I look back and think, "How the heck did I do that day in and day out?" I'm worn out now just thinking about it!

There were markers that I was doing a good job. On our fourth Mom's Day together, Natasha made me a little handprint and glued shells around it. She said it reminded her of the two of us walking on the beach. "You always walk beside me and I will always walk beside you," she said. (I've schlepped that little plaque on my last several moves. It's beautiful and still so precious to me).

Jake appreciated how I mothered his children. "You are my angel," he would tell me.

As much as I appreciated the compliment, I continued to wish that he would finally step up and act as the kind of father I craved for Haley. This was a man who adored his own children, but treated mine like she was outside that loop of unconditional love.

As Natasha grew up, there were other hurdles. She would complain that her bio Mom was not around enough. I would always tell her, "Your Mom is doing the best she can, sweetheart. Your Mom loves you." I truly meant it because compassion was key to raising these kidlets, and I was learning more every day. Deep down, I knew that Exey was doing the best she could under the circumstances, too.

It was still a very happy and charmed childhood. Natasha got her first pony when she was six and I enrolled her into a pony club where she could learn to ride and become a responsible young human. Everyone would mention to Jake and me how wonderful Natasha was to have around because of her natural joy. Each day after school, I'd bring her to the pony club and we shared a love for horses. I even went the extra mile and went camping with her, although this is something that I would not normally want to do. It wasn't my dream to sleep in a freezing cold tent, and the little stinker ditched me for her friends. Back at the campsite, I was covered in dirt and sleeping on the ground while the kids shrieked with joy. I don't think anyone showered for three straight days. I know I'll never wash off those happy memories.

As Natasha grew, she became a fearless rider and quite responsible because she was so in love with her pony. It was another bond between the two of us. At age five, she was also playing on a youth soccer team. In my mind, I can still see that beautiful little girl chasing a fat butterfly down the field. These were such happy days.

I was so content mothering her and thought of my stepdaughter as a gift. I must confess that age made me a more patient mother as the wonder of her childhood unfolded in front of me. I was so happy and delighted – as was Jake – as we watched her grow.

And she did. Kids are tricky that way.

In a breath, she went from that little blue-eyed girl into a full-fledged pre-teenager.

For business reasons, we missed Natasha's graduation from elementary school, arriving a scant fifteen minutes after her name was announced and she collected a diploma. We felt awful. Little did we know that this would be her last graduation.

CHAPTER
FOUR

GREATEST HITS

The real trouble began in middle school when the principal called us in to insist that they wanted to hold eighth grade Natasha back a year because her grades weren't good. Jake fought this idea in a heroic way. "It will be socially traumatizing to have her friends leave her and go off to high school," he demanded in such a way that the school folded – although they didn't think she was ready.

Rules were bent. She was enrolled in Calabasas High School. Jake and I didn't think there would be an issue that a tutor couldn't handle. So, we settled into her first years of high school while Natasha hit puberty in the same way that Haley had many years earlier. Much to her father's displeasure, Natasha was becoming moody and increasingly body conscious. "I'm fat," she would wail to me although it wasn't true. She wasn't boy crazy yet, but she was definitely becoming boy aware.

One day when I was walking around in my riding pants, Natasha looked at me and in an annoyed teenage way said, "Debmama, you've got to get rid of those granny panties." Then she dragged me out to buy some thongs to wear under my clothes.

"They're not going to be very comfortable," I said.

"Yes, they are," Natasha insisted. "You will like them."

And, I actually did.

Jake and I talked constantly about this new time in our lives and he shared with me his take on the psychology of kidlets.

"These kids study us closely. They know our buttons and how to work us." Bingo!

By the time her fifteenth birthday came around, I knew Natasha's hormones were going wild and there would be a whole new playing field and set of rules on how she maneuvered us. The same could be said of Haley who was an older teenager.

The following "greatest hits" were spaced over a three-year period. We would be teased with months of "normalcy" in-between the "hit parade" where Natasha would do astounding things. We were well into a new period of our lives now where I would believe that everything was going to be fine, only to be plunged into another incident a few months later. We would learn later that Natasha is what is called "a periodic addict."

Yes, I said the word.

Addict.

In hindsight, I think they should make a hormone patch for all teenage girls to avoid the looming years of destruction. Think of how much easier it would be without the door slamming, eye rolls or grown temper tantrums – although I'd learn that was the least of it. Natasha's descent was a combination of hormones and hazards that we could never predict. Her fall wasn't measured in giant leaps, but shakey steps toward the danger zone.

As she grew into a beautiful teenager, Natasha had a boyfriend. Okay, great. I didn't like it – and neither did Jake. She no longer wanted me to call her girlfriends' Moms to verify she was really on a legit sleepover either. Score one for the boyfriend.

But not really. Her wishes…. not granted. I still called.

I'd get the wrath, tears and cries of "I'm NOT a baby." All evidence was to the contrary.

She still seemed like my baby to me, but in a nanosecond, she had turned into a not-so-sweet sixteen. The first reality hit me like an earthquake. In a way, it seemed like fate because I prefer the mallet approach as all innuendo and whispering is wasted on me.

"DebMama," she said. "I'm at the principal's office. Can you or Dad come get me right now?"

There was only one problem… or maybe ten.

"Natasha, baby, we're in Vegas. We just got here, remember?" I said. "You're staying at Morgan's house tonight." My stomach began to churn due to the momentary silence on the other end of the line.

"They found some pot seeds in my bag, but it's not mine," she rattled off like this was nothing more than a total misunderstanding. Stupid adults!

Thank God, I thought. Those seeds belong to someone else's child.

I passed the cell phone to her father. "Here, Jake, you talk to her."

It turned out Exey was in town, and we were glad she was on the front lines and could go and rescue our little girl from this obvious misunderstanding.

Upon our return, Natasha told me that her bio-Mom was very upset with her although this was still not her fault.

No kidding. I was upset, too, although my fondest dream was to give our angel the benefit of the doubt. I closed my eyes and pictured the collective parents (all four of us) with our heads together and then all those noggins exploding like giant summer melons.

We were informed that all four parents were actually now required to be present in juvenile ticket court.

Fun reunion!

Natasha was steadfast in her defense. "It was planted on me by girls who hate me," she insisted. In the end, the judge put her in the AA for Kids program. "Stay out of trouble for a year," he told her, sentencing us to what I now call "bad parent" classes.

After attending one "bad parenting" class, Jake informed me he would not be going to any additional sessions. Ok, I would go to the rest on my own. No problem. Uber Mom to the rescue! I remember thinking parents in that bad parent class all seemed so puzzled with their children's behavior. Thank God, none of my children were actually addicts.

The spotlight on my girl was just a temporary mistake.

Or was it?

A few months passed.

We were at home one night. 10 p.m. The shrill ring of the phone startled us.

Jake grabbed it and I had a sinking feeling in the pit of my stomach that there wasn't even a possibility of hanging up with a smile. How can any call coming in after 10 p.m. actually reveal good news? No one calls at that hour to tell you that your child is on the honor roll.

I could hear a rushed voice on the other end and the tone was tinged with pure panic. "Hi, I'm, um, Natasha's friend," said the young girl. "You NEED to, um, come and get Natasha NOW! She's acting… strangely."

Mindlessly, Jake and I drove to the parents' townhouse about twenty minutes away. We didn't have much time to gather the details because Natasha was already coming down the stairs. Once outside, she began to dance away from us until she was swaying and moving up the road.

She refused to get in our car.

In a panic, we saw her boyfriend and asked, "What did she take?"

"Damn it! Tell us!" we demanded.

"A tab of acid…you know, LSD," he finally responded.

Oh my God!

Finally, we managed to persuade an out-of-her-mind Natasha to get into our car and this only happened thanks to her boyfriend who also piled in the backseat. He had also taken the drug, but somehow had avoided the intense reaction Natasha was having now. Thank goodness for small favors.

A rambling stream of words flew out of our baby's mouth as I stared into her round, wild eyes.

"The world is coming to an end! We're all going to die!" Natasha rambled. She went on and on as my brain felt boggled. I'm someone who has never tried acid or LSD and seeing Natasha's reaction to this drug made me thankful that I had refrained.

Even at that moment, I refused to accept the inevitable. Kids try things at college. Maybe she was just getting an early start. She would remember this and never ever do it again ……

Somehow, we got her into bed that night after dismissing the boyfriend. Our sadness lingered and so did our puzzlement. How in the world could our happy perfect baby keep doing such bad things?

We knew there would be consequences because she was under a judge's order for a year, which included random drug testing. In a way, we welcomed this yoke around her neck, thinking it would keep her in check. This was a one-time incident. Who would be silly enough to do drugs while being drug tested?

Natasha would.

It only took a few months for the call to come that marijuana had shown up in her blood stream causing the high school to suspend her for six weeks.

Shit, shit, shit! What do we do now?

Jake and I went around and around. We wanted this moment to be a punishment and a wakeup call. Obviously, the enforced AA meetings hadn't helped her and neither did her school suspension. How was that a true deterrent? Kids her age dream about weeks off from school and I called this an extended summer vacation. Why wasn't extra school the true punishment?

Our ah-ha moment came thanks to Exey who was in England working on a show. "Let's send Natasha to her," Jake said. "It will be cold. She doesn't have any friends there and she will be away from the boyfriend."

I contacted my sister Tish, who still lived in the UK, and asked her if Natasha could come and stay with her as well for a couple of months. Thankfully, Tish, her husband and two boys promised that they would welcome our not-so-little girl with open arms. We just needed to bide our time until we could send her across the pond.

The night before Natasha was due to leave, we found our daughter escaping from our house with a rope made of sheets dangling from her bedroom balcony window. Panicked that she would fall and break her bones, we rushed from the house to catch her. But we were too late. Our front gate, high and huge, wasn't an obstacle either. Swiftly, she climbed over it. It was like watching a prison escape. Or I likened it to watching one of the women from Bram Stoker's *Dracula* movie. She had turned into a human lizard.

"I frickin' hate you guys! Just stay out of my life!" Natasha screamed at us.

She also made one thing clear. She was not going to the UK. I actually remember feeling sorry for my neighbors who couldn't help but hear the loud outbursts.

She could run, but she couldn't hide. Yes, Natasha got on the plane and went away to hopefully get a new perspective. The time passed slowly for us as we desperately missed her. However, the weekly phone calls were assuring – especially when my sister Tish told me, "It's a pleasure to have Natasha with our family. She's a regular sparkle."

My eyes welled up. That was the little girl I knew.

A sparkle of joy.

"Our boys adore her," my sister told me.

Could it be possible that we were waking up from a nightmare that one day we would look back on as simply a blip of time when our precious girl was teetering on a ledge, but didn't fall and crack open?

Weeks passed and the phone calls starting coming from Natasha who once again sounded like the girl we loved. She pleaded with us to come home, sobbing and promising that she would "be good" and had "seen the light and its name was sobriety."

"Dad and DebMama, I just want to come home," she cried.

We missed her so much that we gave in, thinking it would be better now to keep a careful watch on the girl who certainly had an epiphany during her overseas trip. So, we paid to have the airline ticket changed and Natasha came home a week early.

She hugged us tightly and reaffirmed her promise to stay on the right side of the tracks. Another plea came the day she arrived home. "DebMama," she said. "I've missed my friends so much. Please, can I stay at Suzie's house tonight? I haven't seen her for months and she is my bestest friend. It's her 17th birthday and I promise that her mom will be there. Please. Please. Please."

"But we missed you," I implored. "Don't you want to stay with us?"

Natasha was quite convincing. "I do, but I need to see my friends, too. It's just for tonight. Please."

Natasha logged only twelve hours in the United States and was off to stay at her best girlfriend's house with a parent standing watch. Just in case.

"Don't get into any trouble, baby. Okay?" I implored.

"Don't worry, DebMama," she assured me. "I know… I know!" As I stared into those clear, wide and innocent blue eyes that were always so beautiful, my heart longed to believe her. The jury inside my head knew that Natasha was smart and certainly didn't want to return to the rocky times that led to her trip overseas. A reunion with friends sounded like so much fun for her – almost a little welcome home present for cleaning up her act so swiftly.

Fast-forward to the next day Riiiinnng. Riiiinnng!

It was Natasha's stepdad on the line, calling from the UK. "So, we hear that our daughter came back early to America and you guys….." His voice trailed off for a moment due to a bad connection. I heard his next words clearly. "And she has been to jail already -- in less than 24 hours."

Was he insane? Of course, Natasha wasn't in jail. This was just a surreal conversation with a parent who was much too far away to be abreast of current events.

It turned out that he was right. I was gobsmacked! The circle of truth had one loophole that remained open and it involved Jake and me not knowing what was going on. Natasha had been to the police station the prior evening where she had been booked for juvenile criminal activities. Apparently, she didn't just stay home with her best friend on the night of her return. She had gone with several friends to a vacant house where they threw a raging, wham-bam welcome home party for her. The police were tipped and busted all of them, citing beer and cigarettes at the scene of what was now an actual crime.

The police escorted Natasha to the station in handcuffs and immediately booked her and the others on the charges of underage drinking and smoking.

A bright spotlight beamed on her misdeeds, but she still managed to keep even a trickle of that light from us for a good twenty-four hours. As resourceful as ever, Natasha called her Uncle Mathew to pick her up. After swearing him to secrecy under the banner of "kids will be kids," he ended up feeling guilty and placed a call to Exey. From there, the loop of information became ever more bizarre. It pained me to know that they heard about Natasha's adventure in another country before we heard about it in the same town.

There was only one source left. I wanted to hear what happened from my daughter who soon was under our roof again on bail. Explaining herself had become second nature by now. She was very apologetic and did not know they had planned a welcome home party for her.

Our stress level seemed lodged in the red-hot zone and I feared it would stay there permanently before she came of age.

Reason was lost when she batted those baby blues at us. I still loved the sound of her laugh and Jake melted when she professed her deep love for us.

Looking at her, I felt that love. It was enough to convince myself that everything was going to be just fine.

Luckily, life returned to some sort of normalcy. Eventually,

Natasha's suspension from school was rescinded and she resumed her normal teenage life of hitting the books. Natasha loved her teachers and classmates, so it wasn't a struggle to jump back into the familiar routine. Our daughter loved going to school, and despite current affairs, teachers would still tell us how delightful she was to have in class.

Of course, she was delightful. This was our Natasha and her sparkle carried into the outside world.

As for the rest, we would fix her.

An unpleasant task occurred when Natasha and I had to pop into the local police station to get a copy of the ticket she was given for her night of fun at the vacant house. This was not my Mom-daughter outing of choice. At the Lost Hills Sherriff's station, Natasha pointed out a wall of framed pictures of all the officers. "Look, DebMama," she said, singling one out. "This is the officer that came to our school and told us not to do drugs."

I was glad that she had digested this piece of information so well.

"Look!" she whispered. "That's the one who busted us at the vacant house." Her voice was oddly excited, especially when you considered the situation. She pointed to another photo. "And this is the one who put me in handcuffs and made me get into the back of a police car."

The cherry on my cake for this day had been placed. My daughter had run the full gamut from a warning to becoming a cautionary tale.

High school graduation loomed in just four short weeks and all was quiet on the western front. I didn't want to jinx it and said a silent prayer, hoping that things stayed that way. All signs pointed to the positive. Natasha was earning good grades and her teachers still adored her. Something close to breathing normally over our "Natasha Situation" settled into our beings. Kids get into trouble; and kids got out of trouble. The world went on.

That damn phone rang again.

This time it was Natasha's high school principal on the other end, and my stomach did a customary churning as my insides were being wrenched with his every word. He informed me that Natasha's mandatory blood tests came back showing positive for Oxycodone.

What the f*&$ was that? I had never heard of it.

"Natasha is suspended," he explained and then told me that we would soon have a court hearing held by the teacher's school board. He would preside over this hearing and there was no guarantee that she could ever return to school or graduate.

I looked at that phone with utter hatred.

Thus began my aversion to answering anything that rang.

That night, Jake and I researched, but could find no real information on the Internet as to why someone would willingly take this pain medicine. Natasha didn't have a reason either and told us that maybe someone had put it in her drink without her knowledge. The important thing was her future. We wanted her to graduate; Natasha wanted to walk in her cap and gown.

It should have been a happy time of prom and college plans, but instead, we were preparing for a school court hearing that would decide our daughter's future. At the hearing, we went with the "someone put something in her glass" defense." It didn't work. Natasha remained expelled just a month shy of graduating.

Somewhere during this second suspension, I wrote the following in a diary that I started keeping. The book would become a lifeline to pour out my feelings.

When we arrive at the school, Natasha leaps from my car and bounces up the stairs. School is just letting out, and there are lots of shouts from her fellow students, thrilled to see her. The principal is descending the stairs, sending us a big scowl that takes over her face. I understand.

Natasha, my daughter, you are beyond a sparkle. I love you with all my heart, and how could I have done this to you? Natasha, you seem so happy to me most of the time. Why do you need to swallow fricking pills? You are from an addictive gene pool; please don't go the drug route. Your best girlfriend has just been put in rehab. I have an overwhelming urge to put you there, too, make you safe, make you learn drugs are BAD. Jake resists all ideas of this, telling me you are fine.

Fine……….. but suspended for a second time …..I doubt they will let you back, but heck, let's give it our best shot at your hearing.

I am overwhelmed with my feelings of inadequacy.

Steve, the homeschool teacher we met with seems so enamored with your family history from your Mom's side. You must get that a lot. Natasha, and to your credit, you are you and you never trade on what your family lineage is. Natasha, you have been so strong for me, but why do you do this?

Is it because you have a wild, untamed, adventurous 17-year-old spirit?

CHAPTER
FIVE

LIFE COLLISIONS

Just as Natasha traveled down a frightening path, my eldest, biological daughter had a huge surprise for us that made my stepchild look almost angelic.

I haven't mentioned Haley for a while, but now it's time to shine a light on my other beautiful daughter who didn't have an easy road. It must have been shocking to go from having your Mom all to yourself, to suddenly sharing her with a two-year-old baby girl and an eight-year-old stepbrother. Add to the mix a difficult stepfather, and you have a recipe for an internal detonation.

When we had moved out to Malibu, Haley was in high school, which was difficult in many ways. The location was breathtaking, but those tender years don't run by a zip code. Haley had always suffered from learning disabilities and now she had to face the rigors of a new school while trying to make new friends. God had gifted Haley with a stunningly beautiful lampshade, but I know she felt fragile on the inside.

As for her learning disabilities, the pros diagnosed her with Attention Deficit Hyperactivity Disorder, or ADHD. Reading and writing had always been rather impossible for her in the conventional manner. Each year, I would attend an I.E.P. (Individual Education Plan) for my daughter to map out her school year. All the teachers, psychologists and various others attended the meeting as a team versus one of me. I was just The Mom who wanted her baby to learn. Vehemently, I resisted all suggestions that I should put her on medicine knowing I didn't want her to live this way. With hindsight, maybe I should have gone that route.

Memories of meetings past could never be erased. I remember physically flinching when I was told my daughter read at a first-grade level. The only problem was that she had just completed fifth grade.

I'm so glad that there has been so much progress in dealing with special education needs now in the year of 2019. Perhaps that child's reading or writing is different, but so many have such stunning talents in other areas. These children need talented teachers and understanding.

No one could deny that Haley was a very intelligent, gentle, funny and kind girl. She also shared my affinity for creatures. There was no animal, great or small, that she didn't befriend and the those on four legs always loved her right back.

The same could not be said for humans. Haley was also a stunningly beautiful young lady with long brown hair and beautiful brown-black eyes. Even for the beautiful, high school can be a very cruel place for anyone who stands out in any way. If you happen to be very pretty, this is the perfect excuse for viciousness from other girls. They zeroed in on the fact that Haley was in the "learning disabled classroom" and the taunts really flew despite my daughter's heartbreaking wishes to just fit in.

It was such a painful time in her life, and I would have willingly cut off any body part to right the situation for her. Why couldn't I take on her pain and put her on a level playing field with everyone else? Once when I visited her special classroom, I noted that there were no windows and the teachers seemed to just plop these kids in front of a television for big chunks of time.

Haley remained a good kid who tried hard. A brush with truancy was her worst high school offense. I couldn't even be mad when she and her best friend ditched school to go to the beach. In Malibu, what kid didn't do that on a warm spring day? Haley also blossomed into the most incredible horseback rider. No jump was too high. At horse shows, when other young ladies rode their steeds that their parents spent thousands of dollars on, Haley was on "her backyard horse." Her horse was the least expensive one out there, but she had trained him correctly. Her focus and determination shone through and I was so proud of her accomplishments. My daughter was brave and did the right thing. She would never take care of herself until her horse was cared for and safe. No matter how tired she was after a long competition, it was all about the comfort of Tutt, her four-legged love.

These were wonderful traits for a human to possess and I just knew that the partnership my girls had with their horses would ensure that they would turn into fine young adults.

There are many ways of keeping horses and ours were in our backyard. This wasn't stereotypical rich kid stuff, and I loved it. Instead of paying for your horse's care, both girls had to get out there with a shovel and deal with the manure. This hands-on, real life experience taught them priceless lessons about getting your butt out there in the freezing cold or searing heat to look after something that's living. I'd joke to Jake: "Horses are a way cheaper proposition than therapy."

Later, I would change my mind.

I would roam our ranch with the horses thinking back on my earlier life with Haley. She had been christened when she was ten in Montecito, California and her Godmother Susan had helped her pick out a new name: Francis after St. Francis of Assisi. It perfectly fit my daughter as she grew into a lovely young woman.

At 16, a very mature Haley even went to visit her Godmother in Hydra, Greece. I was anxious when we picked her up from the airport because she had been away for three weeks and I missed her so much.

Jake, Natasha and I gathered around the baggage area at LAX and watched all the suitcases roll down. We waited. No Haley.

Panic gripped my heart as my mind raced. Someone must have stolen her, I thought.

"No such luck," Jake would later say.

I had to smile.

On that day, I alerted the airport folks who announced her name again and again over the intercom as her cases spun around on the carousel. Suddenly, the airport arrival room seemed empty. That's when I heard the familiar sound of clip-clopping stilettos across the hard floor.

Haley plopped herself into my arms and I felt a jolt of pure joy.

But wait…she was carrying something. In a container.

Loud meows were coming from the thing. Shit! How could she bring a cat back from Greece? I knew that Jake would explode, as unexpected animals were not welcome.

Natasha and I locked eyes and went into overdrive, covering up the cat carrier with a coat in the back of the car and then we proceeded to talk very, very loudly to cover up the "meow, meow, meow." The gig wasn't up; we made it home and Haley managed to sneak her new friend all the way up to her room.

The cat's name was Hydra. Haley explained how unwanted animals live in a dreadful state in Greece. This was a life-saving mission. Luckily, there were no particular import rules for kittens coming into the United States except for a proof of shots, which Haley had accomplished on her own.

I really don't know when Jake noticed we had a new family member. I'm sure he assumed that Hydra just showed up. In a way, he did.

Haley also surprised me with a new cage in her room. I looked in nervously and said, "What the hell? It's a RAT!" I was absolutely scared stiff.

"Well, does it have a name?" I asked her.

She smiled at me in that beautiful way with her brown eyes sparkling.

"Debbie," she said.

During her graduating year from Malibu High School, we agreed that City College, two hours north, in Santa Barbara, would be an excellent choice for Haley. They had the most advanced wing dedicated to learning disabilities of all kinds. My heart jumped for joy that Haley would find a place suited for her needs. Finally, she would have the technology and teachers that she needed. My goal for her was simple: Haley just needed to be all that she could be.

The excitement of touring the campus, along with meeting another new student to share an apartment, was a wonderful experience. Soon, I was moving her belongings into that apartment and helping her settle in. My job was going well, and I could happily cover all the expenses for Haley each month.

I was excited for her and blissfully unaware of how unprepared she was for this next step.

I couldn't see that my little girl was so lost.

Yet, my little bird left the nest and I lamented that she wasn't very good at keeping in touch with me. Finally, after a couple of months of no word, I was concerned and called the college. "I'm just wondering if my daughter is assimilating into her new life?" I said.

To my horror, I discovered that colleges don't discuss students over the age of 18. Really? The mother in me wanted to scream: "Why the hell not? This is my child!" I reasoned with them that I was paying her tuition and expenses and they insisted that they couldn't violate her privacy.

I drove up to school for a visit. As I walked towards Haley's apartment, I chatted with other students who lived there. They seemed perfectly fine and to be enjoying the college experience. It turns out that Haley was also loving college, but for the wrong reason. It seemed that my daughter was getting an A in partying and had only bothered to grace the school campus twice.

We had our "come to Jesus" moment. Haley cried, "I'm miserable here at college. Please, please, please can I move home?" Oh, how I would have loved to have her back again, but I knew Jake would be wholly against this move. Once again, I found myself tap dancing between my child and my husband.

Haley had a bailout plan that involved moving back to town and going to school in Santa Monica or Hollywood where she would be on her own, but closer to the family. This sounded like the perfect compromise because I could make it work and check on her. All I wanted was for my daughter to be a happy, healthy and productive human being.

I would move her.

Another light bulb moment came when Haley informed me that

she wanted to pursue acting and enroll in those kinds of classes to follow her true passion and calling. It was the same conversation so many parents in California have with their children. I had that talk with my own parents. A spark was lit.

A few months later and Haley was living in a small apartment crammed with every kind of animal she could fit as her companions: two huge dogs, cats, rats, rabbits, and a bird. "They are my family," she said.

I understood.

Haley's acting teacher called me and it was good news. "She's going to be the next Julia Roberts," he said. "She has true talent. I'm going to see if my own agent will represent her."

Finally, I could breathe again. I was so relieved that Haley had found her niche doing something she loved.

Natasha and I even went to watch Haley on stage, and we were blown away at the way she had a large audience laughing. The first time we saw her perform, Haley actually received a standing ovation. The happiness I felt watching my daughter live her dream and find her feet in this world remains one of my fondest memories.

Thinking that Haley was finally on track, I focused on my job, which had actually turned into a career. Beyond busy, I took the leap with my then boss to start our own new firm. The days, months, weeks and years seemed to fly, and time morphed into some kind of blur. We got loans out against our homes and we were off.

We were headquartered in Texas where my partner lived. He was the brains of our organization and was handling the day to day running of our company and our employees. Meanwhile, we needed to get plenty of business to keep us all afloat. I flew all over the United

States now, meeting with the Presidents and CEO's and the legal teams of Fortune 500 companies in order to get new business and service existing clients.

In fact, after just 18 months of business, a fortune 500 company offered to purchase us. Wow, I thought, I really was living the American dream. I came here with nothing and now have employees and a solid company. I chatted with my partner who said, "Well Deb, I really don't want to go back to working for a big corporation."

I agreed that we would remain our own bosses.

In 2007, I would regret that decision.

What I do remember is signing lease after lease for Haley as she kept changing apartments. My God, what would happen if I didn't sign? She would have become a homeless vagrant living in Hollywood. As her mother, I could never let that happen and had to protect her.

Thus, I began years of sending food and rent money each month. I was a one-stop checkbook paying for her gas, electric and auto payments. This was my baby girl and she was struggling to make her dream come true. All that needed to happen was for me to hear her on the phone with catch in her throat. I knew that tears were only a moment away, and that would send me into a flurry of activity to save the day. As always, Haley and I only had each other.

She only had me.

Me. The Enabler Extraordinaire.

I was determined to make sure that life ran smoothly for my child, as I was the wind beneath her wings, as the song goes. This wasn't a job, but my absolute privilege. Of course, there were also reality checks.

"Haley, you must get a job to help pay for your life," I told her.

I think I must have sounded like a broken record. It became my mantra. My daughter was always ready with a slew of excuses. She was too busy with classes and had to learn her craft. Or should I say crafts? Haley wanted to enroll in every kind of class possible to learn a trade.

"Mom, I want to try bartending."

"I can do that at night, so I can audition in the daytime"

And so we tried that idea…… until things changed again.

"Mom, I want to learn how to be a makeup artist."

The school looked so amazing and Haley would be taught how to do special effects make up for film, which could lead to a career.

My credit card was on fire, but always managed to stretch far enough to charge whatever education she needed. It was just money. Wasn't this what responsible parents were supposed to do? Wasn't that why I worked so hard – to give her a fishing rod?

One day the makeup school called and told me that Haley hadn't been showing up and they were going to expel her. I pleaded with them to give her another chance. In the back of my mind, I always thought that if Haley had just "one more chance," she would buckle down and everything would be wonderful.

I would frantically call her each morning, and in a pleasant voice say, "Get up darling! Get ready."

An hour later, I'd call the school to see if she had arrived and then call her again. On and on, my hamster wheel went spinning into oblivion.

I knew that we needed to have a serious discussion, so I drove out to see her. On the way there, I saw Haley and her friend walking down the road. It pained me to see that she was dressed in tattered pants that were literally falling off her bum, plus a ripped shirt and she wore tons of thick makeup. I almost didn't recognize my own daughter.

Where was my young lady? We were British, for God's sake. Wasn't some decorum supposed to just rub off or be implanted in the DNA?

Her landlord called frantically that a week later to tell me that my daughter was housing a pig in her apartment. A pig? "Yes," said the infuriated landlord. "And she won't get rid of it!"

My name was on the lease and on my birthday, I fibbed to Jake and said I was going into town for a birthday lunch with my girlfriends. In reality, I drove to Hollywood with Natasha, who gamely agreed to go with me. This was before her suspension and greatest hits, so the only person I had riding shotgun in that car was the one who brought me pure joy. She was filled with possibilities, as was Haley, or at least I hoped.

Upon arriving, we found Haley in a grumpy and edgy mood. She was extremely skinny while her hair was filthy, and her demeanor remained very hostile. It was clear that the last thing she wanted was a visit from the family. Where was my child? All I saw was this hostile girl and her pet pig.

"Pigs are super smart, Mom, and they can be house trained," she informed me like this was no big deal.

Yes, but they could also result in a health inspection visit. Apparently, I was going to be fined $500 a day until piggy was removed.

In the end, Natasha and I, plus the peeved landlord, had to

wrestle with this heavy pig as we moved him into a cage. Then we had to manipulate that cage into the elevator amid the curious stares from the other inhabitants of this apartment building. Huffing and puffing, we somehow managed to "heave ho" the pig into the back of my SUV.

Haley reacted by having a hysterical breakdown. Sobbing and screaming, she couldn't emotionally handle the loss of her newest pet. Wailing loudly as if her heart was being ripped out, she put on quite the show for anyone in the vicinity. I'm shocked that no one called 911.

Believe me when I say that I didn't discount her pain because it was real. I knew how much comfort this lonely girl got from her animals.

Natasha and I had the task of driving back to Malibu with Jelly Belly – the pig's name – and we delivered him to a local farm that belonged to a dear friend of mine who promised that he would have a lovely life.

Natasha mentioned to me on the drive back home, "DebMama, Haley was not always like this? Remember? She was normal when she lived at home."

I could not remember at that moment as the chaos engulfed every fiber of my being.

"So, how was your birthday lunch?" Jake asked me later that evening – after I showered any trace of the pig off me.

"Great," I said, my tightrope wearing thin as I separated my Haley life with my Jake life. I was an expert in keeping the lid down on both of those boxes. Haley didn't hear about Jake; Jake could never hear about Jelly Belly. I didn't want him to be able to put another chip in the bad Haley pile.

That night, I was restless remembering the foul smell in my daughter's little apartment. Even now, many years later, a specific odor can take me back to less than happy places and times. That animal stench engulfed me the minute I walked through the front door. It was putrid and sick; the smell that attracts flies, and it hit us in waves that almost turned our faces green.

A few days later, I returned to Haley's apartment with Natasha and every cleaning product under the sun. We rolled up our sleeves and got to work. Writing this reminds me of how naïve and daft I was in those years when I remained in my ostrich position. I was so uninformed and never stood still long enough to even learn a new or better way.

My personality would rather scrub my daughter's filth away. Natasha and Haley marveled at how I got through that apartment like a whirling dervish who spent most of the time on her aching hands and knees. It felt as though if I cleaned hard enough, somehow my real daughter would shine through and a fresh start would be in the offing.

The only thing fresh in that room was the bowl of lemons I brought to kill the awful smell.

During the big clean, I found a pile of her horse ribbons, hundreds of them, squished in the bottom of a shelving unit and covered in the foulest cat pee. Haley had always treasured those ribbons and I had to throw them all away. They were a disgusting, clumped mess, which made me so very sad. I felt like I was throwing away part of her – the happy part. I was tossing in the garbage the memories of glorious childhood accomplishments

As time passed, Haley was becoming increasingly angrier with me for no real reason. Our encounters involved an organizing, helping, problem-solving Mom who wanted to rescue a hostile daughter. I found that I wasn't having fun with her and seeing her made my gut

churn in a way that was natural in a high alert situation.

Was it acceptable for me to admit that I didn't enjoy being around my own daughter? It didn't take long for every encounter to end with a violent outburst from her and a venomous stream of hatred directed at me. I began to send money to avoid those situations, reasoning that I was still blowing wind beneath those fragile wings.

My own emotions ran the gambit from excruciating guilt to such sorrow that I cried alone knowing that I couldn't make my daughter happy anymore. Deep down, I knew that Jake would never let her move home – especially not in this condition. I didn't want to ask myself the bigger question: Did I even want her to move home?

When the next lease signing came up, I suggested, "Why not move back to our neighborhood? You can teach horseback riding and leave Hollywood behind. Time for a fresh start."

To my relief, Haley actually agreed.

"Ok Mom, I'll give it a go," she said in a weary tone.

I signed and she moved. I even set about getting her groceries as she was still bone thin and had become weak and unhealthy. I knew I'd work on her weight, but these nasty red spots on her once beautiful face concerned me. It was almost as if she was scarred from what I assumed was extremely poor nutrition.

Now that she was closer, it was easier to see her although there was still something about being in her company that left me feeling uneasy. Maybe it wasn't Haley at all. I was still running in place so fast that I could have made the Mad Hatter jealous.

I was encouraged when a close girlfriend of mine named Ava, reintroduced me to the idea that maybe Haley was a good riding teacher. "Haley was the most talented teacher my girls ever had – bar none," she said. That sentence is still etched firmly in my memory bank because of the source. Ava is a kick-ass endurance horse rider and a take-no-prisoners judge. Her opinion made my heart sing with happiness.

I was so used to making excuses for Haley's "off" behavior that I needed a slice of sunlight. Maybe she did have Asperger's Syndrome and just needed to simplify her life in order to succeed.

I was hopeful during those first few months when she settled into her new apartment by us. In no time, she had many new clients and taught them how to ride and various other aspects of horse care. She even added jumping to the mix. I was thrilled that she found a stable that was positioned in a great location for her to turn this into her new life.

One day, I stopped by and found Haley with baby goats following her everywhere. She had just spent hours planting flowers and even logged time with her own six horses. "I paid for my horses all by myself," she told me with pride in her voice. "I also rescued a few from slaughter."

My baby girl was back!

Hallelujah!

Hope springs eternal and I was always an optimistic soul.

Her "I Love Lucy" moments – as I called them – continued. Yet, each phone call from her seemed to require my credit card because she needed a quick fix of the daily disaster.

"Mom, a golf ball just hit my windshield. I can't see out and I'm going to be late for work."

"Mom, I've run out of gas on the freeway."

"Mom, I just had a car accident; I'm on my way to the hospital."

"Mom, the apartment has flooded."

Even though she seemed generally happy, I always had an underlying sense of panic in my tummy ready to flare at a moment's notice. Praying I would always have enough credit available on my card, I worked extra hard to earn commissions to help keep her afloat.

Did I mention there was a boyfriend – and he moved in with her?

The boyfriend was handsome, tall, charismatic and an ex-champion surfer who was sponsored by a major clothing and surfing company. It sounded promising, but then came the wake-up call. The boyfriend apparently had a car accident a few years prior, which left him with a broken back. He was now forever unable to surf – something, he told me, he sorely missed. I'm sure he did.

His new career options were questionable including a plan to become a tattoo artist. Well, maybe he would open his own store. Or maybe not.

A month later, my beautiful St. Francis of Assisi in high heels showed me a large, extremely ugly tattoo that was etched and inked across her entire back. Apparently, he had decided to use her as his test canvas.

Silly boy, silly girl! Didn't they know it wouldn't wash off?

I was completely gobsmacked as we say in England. Why on earth would any sane person willingly allow anyone to learn how to tattoo on her own skin? My baby's once pale back was now unrecognizable to me.

I had the boyfriend to thank. The surfer tattoo genius.

He had another surprise for me that forever will remain tattooed on my brain.

"Nobody wants to believe their child is a drug addict, but your daughter is one," The boyfriend informed me in a special hand-written note.

His last words: "Haley really needs help."

My knee-jerk reaction: Was he nuts? My daughter was NOT taking drugs. For the first time in ages, she was actually holding down a steady teaching job. Why was he saying these things to me?

I went to the source. "Your boyfriend sent me a note," I said in a rushed voice. "He said you were doing drugs. Are you?"

"Oh Mom, he's the one taking drugs," Haley insisted. "He's on pain medication for his back. He takes more than he should. He's just getting even with me because I told his Dad about his drug problem."

Oh.

Okay. An exhale.

There was some sense here.

My world snapped back into place.

Only I wasn't sure I heard the snap.

The note nagged at me and I wondered whom I could ask about drugs. I didn't know anyone who did them although my world began to tilt on two parallel levels. At this time, Natasha was just starting her "antics," so my learning curve was wobbly at best. I did know that Exey had a great deal of knowledge. She had fought her own demons successfully and had first-hand and quite painful experiences with addiction in her family.

Exey agreed to meet with me to talk about it. She suggested her friend's office because he was a doctor with a long history of being a resource for addicts that needed help.

Natasha went with me to smooth the way between her Mom and her DebMama. I couldn't have loved her more if I had given birth to that precious girl. She even went into battle on my behalf in the parking lot with a very irate man who had a tow truck blocking my car when I wanted to leave. My girl was petite in structure, but I was proud that she could roar like a lion. In fact, I stood there transfixed while she gave him such a mouthful. Supergirl to the rescue!

It was the one bright spot to an otherwise tough day because the meeting had been way too much for my ostrich brain to take in. Again, my head was buried so deeply in the ground that my legs were stretched out vertically and pointed toward the sky.

One word whirled around my brain like I had put my frontal lobe in a blender.

Rehab.

What exactly was rehab for adults? Did it work? I knew she must go willingly. But she's not doing drugs, my mind screamed. This can't be happening to my Haley, my St. Francis of Assisi in stiletto heels. My joyful, nutty, funny daughter was NOT an addict.

I thought of this day as an interesting fact-finding mission that had absolutely nothing to do with me. Yet, I thanked my husband's ex-wife because she had given her time and compassion freely.

On the drive home, I thanked my little warrior who was riding shotgun and breathed a sigh of relief that this meeting was behind us.

I decided to live the mindset of parents who don't want to believe what's happening. I don't need to do anything. Everything is fine.

Life is great as an ostrich.

One footnote. I had the following conversation, word for word, on our drive home. It became my mantra to my girls.

"Natasha, just say no."

"DebMama, I know, I know," came the groan back.

"Drugs fry your brains," I persisted.

"Debmama, honestly," she said with a sigh. "I know that. "

CHAPTER SIX

PIGGIES

It wasn't long before Haley's home that I rented for her became a place for her friends to flop – and some new animals, including more piggies. Why not? I was suddenly paying the entire rent for people I didn't even know who were bunking with my daughter. For the millionth time, I told myself, "No more signing on leases. When the lease is up on this house, I won't sign another. Ever again." I promised myself, proud that I had actually taken an empowering step forward.

Call it one small step for me.

The landlord of the prior home sent me a packet after Haley and company had moved out. It included photography detailing the ruin of his pretty place, which left my stomach in knots. Her "friends" had apparently urinated on the water heater. It went on and on. I felt badly for the landlord and so deeply ashamed. Why would adults behave this way, least of all my beloved daughter?

The question of the hour: Where would Haley live now? One option was that she could flop at someone else's place and share the rent. That way, her name wouldn't be on the lease and I wouldn't be responsible. If that wasn't possible, Motel 6 was an option. I knew she could have dogs there, but certainly not a pig. She was still hysterically upset about being separated from her pigs.

At my wit's end, my brain began to dance. So, I called the "unofficial mayor" of my local area who was in her 70s but could give 20-year-olds a run for their money. She also produced a local horsey newsletter each month. Strong and opinioned, she did not suffer fools.

I explained that I was looking for a foster home for the piggies for a bit – at least as long as it took my daughter to find a new home. To my absolute astonishment, she revealed that she had a dog run on her farm, a pen of sorts, and would be willing to give the pigs a try there.

This was one of those moments when gratitude just washed over me. It wouldn't be the first moment – or the last on this journey.

The one condition was that my daughter would need to appear daily at her farm to clean out the pen. It wasn't long before I would hear tales of my daughter appearing in stiletto heels, never on time, to shovel her pigs' manure. I would have loved a picture! Apparently, Haley also learned how to coil a water hose correctly. I didn't know you could coil it incorrectly.

Our pig savior called me after a few days with bad news. Coyotes had been terrifying the piggies at night despite the fact that she would go outside in the pitch black, dressed in PJs, to shoo the predators away. Apparently, they were licking their lips in anticipation of a pork dinner.

When I saw Haley, she was a study in contradictions. One minute, she was so loving, hugging and saying just the right words. The next,

she was hostile and angry. I was never sure which Haley would be wearing those sky-high heels.

Eventually, Haley collected her pigs in her pickup truck and dropped them off at my house. My husband wasn't exactly pleased with anything to do with Haley let alone the piggie drop-off. He felt as if his stepdaughter caused only upset and pandemonium. It's not that he was wrong, but I still went on the defense because this was my baby. I would always spring to her defense.

Again, it was Mom to the rescue. I already had a makeshift pen in the middle of the horse field on our property. I draped every piece of tarp, towel and blanket around the outside fence until it took on the look of a strange, colorful festival. Meanwhile, the horses snorted loudly their objection when it came to their new piggy houseguests. I convinced myself if I tied everything with balling twine – my go-to fix for everything – the pigs would be convinced that the wall was solid. Right?

Hours after my impromptu construction worker act, I collapsed into bed.

It's good to know that even when your world is falling apart, there can still be moments that make you laugh.

The following morning at 6 a.m., the phone rang, and my husband's voice came through the line and directly into my head causing my panic button to flash red alert – my new daily state.

"Deb, do you know anything about the two pigs walking around out here?" he said.

"I'll be right out," I stammered, rushing to get my robe. Racing to the piggies in the backfield, I said a silent prayer that I wouldn't find a disaster waiting for me. I was practically hyperventilating when I saw that the wall didn't hold. For the next hour, I chased the fricking pigs around the property. One thing about pigs: they move like pink race cars. And their squeals of delight as they elude you are blood curdling.

My neighbor even called to see if anyone was being murdered!

"Nope," I replied. "Just life on the ranch."

My husband stuck his head out of his office every ten minutes, and in an extremely put out voice inquired, "Have you caught them yet?"

Did I look like a woman who just completed a pig roundup successfully? I was dripping sweat and my frown said the rest. Close to passing out from the running, I called for Natasha who was blissfully unaware of the chaos outside. She had been enjoying the carefree sleep of a teenager on summer break and I ousted her from her bed. She joined me in her pajamas and Uggs, as I begged for her to hurry to the garden.

Round two of the mad chases began again, complete with bobbing and weaving, followed by more blood curdling squeals that sounded, well, like some pretty rambunctious pigs.

One pig was corralled, but not exhausted.

"Nooooooooooo," I began to scream as Miss Piggy did a racing dive into the deep end of our pool.

"OMG!" I screamed. "He can't swim! Natasha, jump in and save him! Jump in now!"

In one fluid move, Natasha launched her body into the freezing water, Ugg boots and all. She really was my hero. God knows I didn't want to jump in. The funny thing was that the pig had instantly taken to swimming, but still accepted help when Natasha guided him to the steps.

Natasha was soaking wet and cold. She was also furious and let me know how her big sister was a major pain in the ass. There were some other choice words that I won't repeat.

My husband stuck his head out of the office. Almost on cue, he asked, "Have you caught them yet?"

Exasperated, exhausted and with adrenaline coursing through my veins, I replied, "The pigs will be roaming free, wherever they like, for the rest of the day."

In other words, "Bite me."

Of course, Haley appeared at the end of the day after the adventure was over. She was hostile, extremely skinny and stiff like a board when I tried to hug her. Her eyes were glassy and dull. She had no time for reunions with her Mom. Instead, she called for her pigs and to my astonishment, they were like the best trained dogs and came on command. Quite willingly, they loaded into their crates and she left with them.

Her visit consumed an entire five minutes.

A strange relief washed over me. Thank God, she was at least dealing with the pigs. Once again, I fought to find the positive and marveled at her natural gift with animals.

I began to call her St. Francis of "No Fixed Abode" during her Motel 6 stay. If only Haley could have her own patch of land somewhere for her animals to roam, then we could write the happy ending.

As for the pig incident, only one person didn't find it the least bit funny.

And I was married to him.

I searched for some sort of lasting calmness in my life. I was also looking for solutions and found one online when an ad caught my eye: "Mansion On 40 acres. Come Share My House." I called Haley and gave her the phone number, desperate to make her responsible for herself.

"I'll check it out," she promised.

The pigs were living in their crates in the back of her truck. I couldn't imagine her pulling this off. A few hours later, I received an overjoyed phone call from Haley who had visited the property. "The landlord is super nice," she gushed. "I can even bring my pigs and dogs!"

I was impressed with her efforts.

I was grateful for God's divine intervention.

There was more to tell. Haley informed me she was now on Motel 6's official undesirable list.

I didn't ask why. I didn't even want to know why.

CHAPTER
SEVEN

HAPPY OSTRICH OUT OF THE SAND

A few weeks passed and all seemed well. I even visited Haley at her new home, but was puzzled that not much unpacking had taken place. I knew that I could power through a major unpacking in one day and I would work straight until the task was completed. "It's awfully lazy Haley," I said. "Why don't you just unpack already?" When I mentioned it, she would just glare at me.

With Haley in a safe home I could finally take charge of my own life. I could focus on work again including a business trip to Colorado where I had to attend a convention for a week.

A successful convention came to an end and I returned home with a long list of things to get done. This included a needed trip to the hairdresser where I would return my roots to blonde, sit back and relax.

Those were famous last words.

Just as I settled into one of those big beauty shop chairs, glossy magazine in hand, my cell phone began to buzz.

"This is Justin, your daughter Haley's new landlord."

Instantly, I loved Justin because he was the kind of young man that any parent would like as a son or dinner date for their daughter. He was healthy, athletic and well-spoken, which was impressive. He kept talking and talking into my ear as the blow dryers buzzed in the background.

"Your daughter has been doing drugs nonstop since she moved in. Her boyfriend is here too, doing drugs with her," Justin said in a matter-of-fact voice. "My best friend died of a drug overdose and I can't just sit around and do nothing.

"I can't be around this," Justin stated.

"What drug is she on?" I whispered.

"Crystal meth," he said, "Her boyfriend's shooting up on heroin."

Those last two words went off like bombs. What followed sounded like it was said underwater. "I need her out of here, ASAP," Justin demanded.

"She needs a hospital. Some help," he said. "She's killing herself."

Another bomb burst into the air.

The happy ostrich was finally forced out of the sand. I bolted upright out of the chair; stomach punched, and finally turned the corner of acceptance. This earth- shattering phone call was about to change all of our lives, which probably dear reader, you saw coming a million miles away. Believe me when I say that it's far easier to ostrich your life away than accept the brutal truth about your children.

Hear no evil. See no evil. Accept no evil.

Until you're forced to accept it.

The air in my lungs seemed to seep out in a rush as white-hot panic filled my veins with free-flowing adrenalin. My heart was in some sort of vice that was aggressive and unrelenting. Chaos was engulfing me.

In this moment, the only "cover" I had was that I was still blissfully unaware of what a devil named crystal meth can do to a human being. I just knew that it was bad.

Racing home, I made a beeline for my computer and emailed a friend who might know what to do. My fingers could barely type because they were shaking and the rest of me felt numb. I wrote this friend to ask if she knew anyone that I could talk to about meth.

I was absolutely moved and grateful for the Emails that I got back.

God does send angels when you need them and mine were located on earth.

Jackie, my dear friend from Santa Barbara, wrote that she had been showing properties a few days earlier to a chap who was going to start a rehabilitation for all humans in pain. She wrote, "Do you want me to reach out to him and see if he could chat with you?"

"Yes, please," I wrote back as the desperation now coursed through my system. I prayed to God and vowed I would be better. Please, please, please send me wisdom. Help. A plan of some sort. How can I rescue my tortured child?

The answer came from Jackie. Yes, I could call him. In a blink, my newest earth angel went by the name of John Stenzel. He was truly my savior during this time. He was so giving, kind and truly asked for nothing in return.

He was my lifeline, and I drew strength and courage from him. At the same time, he never judged my parenting skills or me. I expected to be judged harshly. It was amazing that John, plus so many others, went out of their way to shower me with kindness when they didn't really even know me.

During our first phone call, it wasn't like walking on glass. I felt as if a firm ground was back under my feet. He told me that the first step was an intervention. I would need to assemble friends to speak to her alongside of an experienced interventionist. Deep down, I had a bizarre feeling we were talking about some kind of witchcraft.

"Is money an object?" he asked.

Blunt. I appreciated it.

"Well, yes, it is," I said.

Molding the situation as if it were fresh clay, he told me about a good friend of his who was an intervention specialist with worldwide success. He would see if she could bring her price down to a fraction of what she normally charged.

A dire moment such as this required magic and I got mine. Things began to fall into place over a life-changing, hectic, four-day period.

John again.

"Ms. Pat Moomy will do the intervention at a lesser price. Call her right now, Deb," he said.

A four-letter word flooded my mind.

Hope.

I loved that Pat was no nonsense and cut through the BS like a steak knife going through butter. "We need to assemble friends for an intervention training this Sunday," she said. "We'll do the actual intervention the next day on Monday."

The following emails are from friends and I began to receive them the minute I put out a cry for help. Their communication was my own lifeblood in this moment.

From Rachel; to Deb:

Dear Deb,

Just spoke to Marie and heard the distressing news about Haley. I'm so sorry to hear it, for both of your sakes and everyone (people and animals) involved. Please know I am here for you, if there is anything I can do to help you, both as a friend and as someone who has a medical and psychological background and someone with different animal connections. Of course, you are off the BBQ duties, so tell me if there is anything for that you need me to take over. Don't worry about Emailing the waivers; we'll just have to make copies and have people fill them out Saturday.

First of all, I highly recommend Dr. J for you (your sanity and to make a plan of action or inaction). He is a psychiatrist, who is affiliated with a hospital and he is very good with medication (if needed), addictions, and couples, as well as individual counseling. I also know people who have had to send their children to special rehab type programs (for similar and different problems), both in state and out of state. I can call and get you names and numbers if you'd like. As far as Haley's menagerie, I can put the word out to see if anyone could foster her dogs if you give me their information. I know of a farm animals place in Moorpark I believe that perhaps would take the goats, sheep and pigs.

I have a friend who is about to start an equine therapy ranch in Arizona, so I can put a feeler call into her for the horses. As for Sebastian, (Haley's prize horse) if you want to try to preserve him for her, perhaps you could board him somewhere for the time being and find someone nice to lease him to in order to alleviate the expense and give him the love and attention he deserves.

Concerning Haley: This is going to be a long hard haul for you both, as I'm sure you realize. For your sake and hers, out-of-state might be a good option. It would get her away from her "bad" connections, remove her from her losses, and keep you at a bit of a distance to not get constantly "roped in." See what Dr. J. or whomever you see says. This is what a friend of mine had to do. This drug is very addicting, hard to ditch and eventually very debilitating from all I hear. I had a brother on it and another who also has similar problems.

I hope you don't mind me saying all this. Just want you basically to know I'm here and willing to help with what I can, as I can only imagine how overwhelming and heart-wrenching this news must be for you and your family.

Sending you strength and love,
Rachel

From Jackie; to Emma:

Hi Emma rec'd this sad email from Deb & just spoke with her on the phone. I have offered to go down & participate in an intervention for Haley if needed & I told Deb I would contact you too about this... nothing has been arranged, but I want to support Deb in dealing with this...

Hope you're doing ok-

Love, Jackie

From Emma; to Jackie:

Gosh, this is so sad, and it is going to be incredibly hard on Deb and Jake getting through this. Naturally, I will help in any way I can. Haley and I get along well. When Haley is stronger, she could consider living in SB for a while (away from her current friends) or at least stay with me for a few days. My friend is a horse trainer at a busy barn and perhaps could consider Haley for work.

I am also more than happy to spend some time with Haley for moral support/friendship or whatever may be helpful. She's a lovely young lady and I would love to assist in any way in which I may be deemed helpful. Feel free to pass this on to Deb whenever you feel the timing is appropriate and let me know if there is anything I can do to help now. Yes, I am up for tough love as you know and will do whatever I can to help Haley and support and assist Deb.

I'm glad you told me about this, and I hope I can help in some way.

Lots of love,
Emma

From Jackie; to Deb:

Hello Deb:
Hope you're feeling a little better… Here's Emma's response to my email. Let us know how we can help, sweetie.

Love,
Jackie

CHAPTER EIGHT

INTERVENTION

At lunch with my best girlfriend Marie, I found myself spilling my guts. She is drop-dead gorgeous, athletic and tall with thick, flowing, blonde hair and the greenest eyes I've ever seen. She also has a kick ass sense of humor that I needed in that moment along with a self-deprecating way of looking at herself and the world around her.

Clear thinking and intelligent, her daughter is a few years younger than Haley. Thinking back, Queen Boadicea heading into battle could not have asked for a stronger soul beside her.

Marie took on her role as my champion Warrior Princess. She also did small things that meant so much including giving me a bracelet that looked like an old-fashioned cuff. Marie told me whenever I wore the bracelet, I would be filled with courage and able to do the right thing.

I should have been born with it on.

At that lunch, we were simply chatting about a local party the next day that we had helped to plan. All the horse folk would attend, and under normal circumstances, I would have been delighted that the day was near to see my friends. After I told her about Haley, I questioned if I should even go to the party although it seemed like a Godsend because I could just lose myself for a few hours. Those brilliant green eyes filled with compassion and she told me to attend. She also reminded me that she was there for me . . . come what may.

Thank God.

Meanwhile, I phoned Haley's roommate to let him know we would be arriving early on Monday to do the intervention. I found out that meth addicts are more likely to be asleep in the early morning hours and you can catch them in an unsuspecting state, as they will certainly be exhausted from the previous night's antics.

Meth addicts. The new vampires.

He told me that he would let her boyfriend know, so they could both make sure that Haley was there. Apparently, her boyfriend was also eager for my girl to get the help she needed. How could he know that she needed this help and I didn't? Oh right, he already wrote me the letter a year ago.

I emailed my friends: "Please could you drop everything and be here, at my home, on Sunday afternoon for the intervention training and then Monday morning for the actual deed?"

Everyone said yes.

Relief flooded through me despite the words of my beloved husband who insisted that no one on my list was doing this for Haley. "They're doing it for you, Deb," he said, quietly.

Really? Was that supposed to make me feel better?

Slap some more lousy on already lousy enough.

I was constantly going back and forth on the emotional scale. One moment, I felt super organized as I learned everything possible during my crash course on rehab facilities from John who was a master teacher. The next minute, I thought I might buckle. At least, there were tasks that kept my mind occupied including making arrangements, faxing medical records, dealing with payment and travel plans. When the pieces began to fall into place and the rehab that would help Haley became real, I was ready to drop to my knees in gratitude.

There was also the issue of her beloved animals. She had two pigs, two huge dogs, rabbits, cats and several horses. What the hell was I supposed to do with them? It turns out that my new friend named Rachel was soon to be the champion of the homeless herd. She was another relative of St. Francis of Assisi. Thank you, God, thank you!

From Deb to John:

Thank you soooooo much for your voicemail. Pat is going to charge me an hourly rate which makes all of this possible. We are having the intervention training this afternoon, Sunday, at 4 p.m., and then the intervention at 8 a.m. Monday (tomorrow) morning.

I have booked Haley into the Pasadena Recovery Center. Please pray for her. She used to be such an awesome girl and an absolute lover of all animals/strays and a talented horse rider and teacher. Please also pray for me to find the strength…

Take care,
Deb

SUNDAY

On the day of the intervention training, my girlfriends Jackie and Emma drove down to me, literally putting their entire busy lives on hold. Why? They considered my daughter's needs to be more precious than anything else in the universe. Marie, Rachel, Ava, Jackie and Emma were there as was my business partner Steve who flew out from Texas. Of course, Jake was to be by my side at the intervention training.

Pat decided it would be better if Jake wrote Haley a letter instead of attending the actual intervention on Monday. His relationship with her wasn't great, and he was more than happy to be excluded from that activity. I couldn't blame him as I was also filled with dread.

Natasha wanted to come to the intervention and participate in the training. She also wanted to write her sister a letter.

"DebMama, Haley wasn't always like this," Natasha reminded me again.

"Remember?"

This was becoming her mantra to me.

Remembering was like a rope that prevented me from drowning.

Images flooded my mind as I fought back the tears. I searched my mind's photo album for a picture of my girl when she was little and innocent with her ponies packed going to a new home, but it was just too painful.

Once the angel squad of participants was in place, we sat around a very large table with our notebooks open and our ears hanging on Pat's every word. Natasha excused herself and headed to her bedroom.

That afternoon, I learned that Haley would more than likely fixate on me. I was to keep my eyes steady, never leaving hers, no matter what transpired. All of the members of the group were told that they must stay focused and stare at her. We would read our letters …one after another.

Jake kept leaving the table, which struck me as rather odd. Finally, I excused myself to find out why he couldn't sit in there with me. His problem was Natasha who was with a friend in another part of the house.

Natasha was drunk.

The first thought that flew through my mind: Dear God, how could she do this to us …now? She was doing this in front of our dearest friends as they planned her stepsister's intervention! This was insane. A furious Jake demanded that Natasha stay in her bedroom, forbidding her to come out and join us. I still have no idea how he kept her in there for the rest of the afternoon. Frankly, I didn't have it in me to deal with her at that moment.

I spoke to God.

"Two at a time?"

Marie would later tell me, "Yes, because God knows you are strong enough."

Did Natasha have absolutely no mercy? We later realized that she got rip roaring drunk to the point of staggering around the house. Can you even imagine planning for your eldest child to go to rehab while the youngest one is getting drunk within your own home? Maybe I could get a two-for-one deal at rehab?

Was there a rehab for Moms who could easily go over the edge?

MONDAY

I didn't need an alarm clock. Adrenalin woke me and my eyes popped wide open. Why couldn't it just be a normal day when I might be off to Starbucks to meet my friends? Instead, I would make coffee and then join my group of earth angels on our mission to save a young woman: my daughter. Marie drove Rachel, Natasha (yes, she insisted on going) and I while Steve rode in his rental car. Jackie and Emma were together in another car. I thought of our little procession as brave souls in flight.

Around twisting roads, we drove to a mansion that sat high on a mountain. The bendy route was about three miles of steep climbs and single track, but I paid no attention. I had no idea what we would do if someone drove right at us from the other direction. Prayer seemed to be the theme of the day.

Haley told me that elephants used to live here on the property. But, of course, they did. The place was an amazing wonderland.

We didn't have time for the usual tour. Instead, we parked our cars and I was amazed that the inhabitants of the house hadn't heard us as our cars pulled up. Pat, our fearless leader, swung opened the front door wide and we all tiptoed inside. We had been told not to speak until after our letter readings and I forced myself to follow the plan.

Just like that. The time was now.

Pat rapped on the huge wooden door that marked Haley's bedroom. There was silence, so she rapped again.

"Who's there?" It was the sound of Haley's muffled voice.

"I'm a friend of your Mom's," Pat said.

"How do I know that? What the fuck do you want?" Haley yelled.

I whispered to Pat, "Tell Haley you have money from me to give to her."

Pat nodded.

"I have money your Mom asked me to drop off to you."

As if someone had shouted ABRACADABRA, the huge door swung open.

On cue, we all swarmed into the room and surrounded the bed.

Back in bed and pulling the sheets up below her chin, Haley rose up on her knees on the mattress. She was indignant and hissing, her black doll eyes staring madly at us. I swear I could see snakes circling her head and woven around her arms like she was a modern-day Medusa. She didn't skip a beat and quickly obscenities poured out of her mouth. Her words were venomous and filled with hatred.

This didn't feel like an intervention to me, but actually more like an exorcism as we steadily read our letters to Haley while she swore, vile words filling the room. She also hissed and remained on her mattress like a trapped animal. As Pat had warned me, the majority of her hatred was directed straight at me. At some point, Steve moved away from the bed because he had the presence of mind to remember that one of us was supposed to confiscate her car keys. This would bring a new wave of cursing later on.

Pat, who was clearly in charge, asked, "Wouldn't you like to live in a nicer way?"

Haley spat back, "What's wrong with this room?"

Let me count the things that were wrong with that room. Imagine the worst drug movie you've ever seen and that was the state of this room. It was pure squalor with open cans of dog food, discarded take out bags filled with rotting food and half eaten pizzas that served as ash trays for cigarette butts. There was shit everywhere.

Finally, Haley had enough and jumped out of bed to make a run for the bathroom. We all knew she wasn't going anywhere far. We were on top of a freaking mountain and she didn't have the energy to climb down it.

I haven't mentioned the other head that was under that blanket. It finally popped out from the other side of the bedding, as we collectively jumped. It was the boyfriend who was concerned, but with a sleepy smile asked if we could turn our backs while he put clothes on.

Emma begged him, "You have to 'out her' when we ask if she's doing meth. You're our only hope."

Emma later confided that Haley gave such a good acting performance during the intervention that it almost had her convinced that she was clean and sober while I was nuts. I guess those acting lessons paid off.

It didn't take long for the party to move to the great outdoors. Haley actually did plan an escape and was found climbing a tall boulder. She refused to come down from her rocky perch and I was told to stay in the shadows, as my mere face seemed to set her off. Even from her new location, she wanted a cigarette and The Boyfriend obliged.

Afterwards, he told me that he was supposed to turn himself into jail on the past Friday, so now there was a warrant out for his arrest. He just wanted to help her get into rehab before he went away. The truth was he had taken a huge chance in waiting to turn himself in past his "due date."

If this was a movie, it now starred an unlikely hero and an extremely pissed off heroine.

Soon, it was just Pat, Natasha and the boyfriend talking to Haley while she remained high above them on her boulder, some thirty feet in the air. There was a beanie pulled far down on her head while the rest of her waist length black hair was whipped around by the wind. I saw her skinny body shaking. I really don't remember how much time passed as the entire situation qualified as an out of body experience.

Pat continued to talk to Haley and eventually a deal was struck. She would be willing to go to rehab if the boyfriend went with her to "check her in". She also wanted him to drive with her. Her other declarations included that she refused to talk to me, drive with me or speak to me ever again. The boyfriend agreed to go on this field trip, and once again, I felt such gratitude to my new unlikely hero.

Off to rehab they went. In my heart of hearts, I knew they could glue her back together.

Of course, we all followed them to the Pasadena Recovery Center (PRC) because I wasn't sure if she needed a parent to sign for her treatment. PRC had been another miraculous gift courtesy of John's recommendation. So many places informed me that the drug addict must be willing to go to treatment. PRC's stance was that they didn't care if I hit her over the head with a mallet. As long as she marched through those front doors and her feet hit the carpet of the reception area then the help would begin. That was my kind of solution.

Once we arrived, Marie actually hid me in her back seat under a blanket. From that vantage point, I could see my darling daughter experiencing her rocky beginning at this place. Like a shot, she was out of the building and running down the road in impossibly high stilettos.

Marie told me not to worry. "She won't get far in those shoes. And where can she go? She has no money. No cell phone." This made sense, so I went back into hiding.

The entire day was so surreal, and I kept having to remind myself, "This is my reality and I needed to stay in the saddle at all costs."

Eventually, Haley gave up and was given a room at the PRC. It turns out I did need to go and sign her paperwork. The nurse told me how sweet the boyfriend was with her. Apparently, in-between his heroin nods, he had been telling Haley how lucky she was to be alive. "I wish it was me in here, too," he told Haley. "But it's you. And you have to do this rehab to get clean. Be strong."

Later, dear Marie was so touched by his heroics she agreed to drive him home to his parents' home in Malibu. I was glad she had enough seats for all of us. On that ride, Marie even questioned him about how drug addicts function in a relationship.

"Haley is lucky," he said. "She has a group of MILF's surrounding her."

Even I had to smile. "I like to call them angels," I replied, adding, "You're brave, Paul. Now, you need to be strong and figure out your own life. Thanks for helping to save Haley."

People make mistakes, but the goodness was shining from this young man. He was determined to do the right thing for my girl, and my heart ached for him and for all the tortured drug stolen souls.

I even forgave him for mutilating my daughter's back with his street art.

The Intervention letter from Haley's stepfather read to her on the day of the intervention:

From Jake to Haley

Dear Haley,
I hope this intervention helps to open your eyes and make

you realize how desperately you need professional help. Your Mom has tried everything she could to help you, but it's just not possible for her to accomplish that on her own. She has been like a wave being smashed into a rock over and over again. Your condition and behavior has caused her more pain and anguish than you will ever know. I know I have been less than the ideal father figure to you, but I love your Mom very much and I can't bear her being beaten up and berated by you over and over again. It's more than I can bear. I truly hope the help you will now get will really have a dramatic and positive effect on you and that one day soon, we can be friends.

Yours,
Jake

A word from the interventionist following up on Haley's admittance to the hospital

From Pat M. to Deb:

Dear Deb,

I will include Dr. M's (Haley's Dr.) # when I fax the assessment over this morning. After you talk to Paul's Mom, find out if he went to jail on Monday night. It was interesting; when he was under the covers at the intervention, he heard everything. Outside he said to me, "Intervention. I like that and the way it was done." He may need to be surrounded by loved ones and hear positive messages as well. Maybe his Mom could think about an intervention the day he gets out of jail, before he can use again. Anyway, we can talk about that later. I just might think about putting what you said on my site. Sometimes I am a little modest and then my husband reminds

me it's ok to share the praises.
Stay well.
Pat

From Deb to Pat M.:

Bless your heart.

Paul was in jail before but did not change his heroin habit and he has such a good soul. So many tortured people walking around. It just makes me sad beyond words. Haley has also been calling Dr. M. Dr. M has only known Haley since she has been using, and I am sure he can see her spiraling out of control. Dr. M lost his son to drugs, and does wonderful work helping troubled children/teens because he cares so much. He also tends to make excuses for behavior. (Much like myself, I mused.)

Apparently, he had told her it was fine to self-medicate with meth!!!!

If you want to put what I said about the experience with you at the intervention on your website, please feel free to do so. I meant every word and more.

I am off to pack up her room today :)
Respectfully yours,
Deborah Richards

From Deb to Haley's boyfriend's parents:

Dear Bruce,

I would love to chat with you and Mary. I really, really know firsthand what you have been through and continue to go through. Haley is in the Recovery Center where she will remain until well. Then she will live at their halfway house in a sober living facility. She will learn life skills including how to support herself and how to be a nice human. The alternative? She will live under a bridge. I have bottomed out on my enabling behavior.

At any rate, my friends and I were so proud of Paul; he literally saved Haley's life by "outing" her. At the recovery center, they asked me if I would like a two for one, as they could see your son was coming out of a heroin stupor.

My insurance covers Haley fully for the first month, and I am making payments after that, I know this is the end of the road, so she has to choose to save herself. My friends and I would be there if you would like to do an intervention for Paul. I really think with a nudge, he is ready for help.

Please let me know if Paul is in jail and when he will be out and please let me know if you would like more information. Your son is bright and so capable. He was so brave for my daughter. Well, you know this about your son. I am here for your family. Big hug to you and your wife.

Love, Deb.

CHAPTER NINE

SAVING THE ANIMALS

L ife after the major moment went on. There was still a Tuesday the following day after the intervention and the cleaning up of Haley's latest life to be done. Everyone was emotionally wiped out and I had a long list of things I needed to gather and drop off at the rehab.

"No mouthwash."

That was a directive that stuck in my mind and I wondered why.

Meanwhile, I headed back to the mansion on the hill and Haley's former home to deal with "the others." Rachel, the animal angel, had been there for long hours the night before feeding, watering and caring for Haley's animals. It turns out that the pigs were endearing and were even able to climb the stairs. Her dogs, Maverick and Bono, and the pigs were friends and hung out as huge, loving, bouncing beings. These were such gentle and loving animals that greeted us with trusting wags and lickings of the face. Oh, my heart was breaking. What would become of them?

Maybe I could keep the dogs because they were like my grandchildren, but I'd need an okay from Jake. I'd ask him later that day.

One of our tasks was to clean up the garage and move all the furniture from her room. We also needed to get the areas sanitized. Steve warned me to keep an eye open for stray needles, so I wouldn't unwittingly stick myself.

The physicality of moving that furniture reminded me of hard labor, but in a strange way it felt good to do something mindless. It felt like penance. Looking back, I don't know how we did it. I decided that any clothes that were decent would hit the Goodwill bags. We didn't finish cleaning until well past midnight.

Out of bed at the crack of dawn the next day, I went out to the stables to try and find homes for her horses, move her jumps and empty her shed crammed with stuff. It felt so unrelenting and as if the tasks would never end. Luckily, there wasn't time to feel badly for myself. Onward we go.

It was only day two in rehab and I got a sad report that Haley had already managed to borrow contraband in the form of a charged cell phone. She was calling everyone and anyone, begging them to pick her up and take her out of rehab.

"My Mom has gone insane and locked me away," she wailed to no avail.

This was all about tough love, and I was learning how to dish it. It still wasn't easy because one slip and I could easily allow my emotions to turn me into the weakest link.

I found solace in helping her animals. A chap at the stables promised to try and find suitable homes for the herd of horses, as there was no way I could afford their board. Again, I wanted to take a moment to wallow and feel sorry for myself, but there wasn't a moment of downtime. There was just the moving of endless things and beings…heavy, endless and shifting life forms.

A spark of bright light entered my world when Rachel told me that she had a friend who wanted to adopt the pigs and could pick them up the next day at the mansion.

It turns out the lady had a brand-new Mercedes SUV, plus two small children in it. She backed her car up to the guest house where the pigs were currently residing in luxury. There were no signs of the friendly piggies of a day ago. Instead, they transformed themselves into loud, squealing and squirming pigs. I thanked my lucky stars that she was also a horsewoman and got down on all fours with me.

I pushed; she pulled. Somehow, we got them into their cages. I was becoming an expert piggy wrangler even if it did take us two hours of grunt work – pardon the pun – to get them in there. I'm so glad the new mom didn't give up on loading them. I knew in my heart that they were going to a great and loving home.

The dogs were another challenge. Maverick and Bono were darlings, but I was forced to place them at the local doggy kennels with an incredibly kind owner named Anna. She told me that it was indeed possible for any new potential parents to come and meet the dogs there. I was a sobbing wreck by this point because I adored those dogs, but Jake didn't want them.

I pleaded, cajoled and begged my husband to let me keep them.

They were such loves, and in spite of their big size, they still loved to curl up on your lap like a little pup. Haley's animals certainly had wonderful dispositions. I couldn't understand why we couldn't keep them, but he was firm in not wanting more pets.

A month and then two passed with no potential adopters. We put up fliers everywhere, but there were still no takers. With a heavy heart and a worn-out credit card, I had to fetch the dogs from the kennels and move them to a local animal shelter. They promised me at the shelter to call if it ever got close to them being put to sleep, so I could collect them. And yes, they would try to adopt them out together.

In that moment that I left them at the shelter, I felt absolute, pure hatred for my eldest daughter. The vortex of collateral damage that had surrounded Haley extended to these most innocent of beings.

Rachel continued to work the impossible with the cats and rabbits that were all successfully placed in super loving homes.

I remain forever grateful.

Animal Rescue Note to Editor of a Local Newsletter

Dear Editor,

As you may be surmising, these animals belonged to Deb Richards' daughter Haley. She has just entered a rehab program and has a long haul ahead of her, as does her Mom and family. These animals need good, permanent homes. Any help you could give Deb with this, i.e. massive emails and word-of-mouth would be so greatly appreciated. The situation is fairly desperate. Luckily, yesterday, we found homes for two pot-bellied pigs, one rabbit, and two of the cats. The goats and sheep are taken care of now. Two dogs (fantastic dogs), one cat, two ponies, and five horses are the ones now needing our help. Thank you so much for whatever you can do to help. We do not need to mention Deb or Haley or rehab; we can just say person is ill and can't take care of her animals anymore.

With sincere thanks,
Rachel

One day, the gentleman from the stables called to let me know he had been able to place six of the seven horses. I could not let the seventh horse go, our beloved Sebastian. He was my other grandchild and I too loved him so. I would not be asking for my husband's permission to keep him; I just simply couldn't.

Haley adopted him as a two-year-old stallion. When she first invited me to meet him, I was absolutely dumbstruck. He was super tall and gangly, as he waited to grow into his baby bones. He was also wild in those days. I thought for sure he would kill her or someone else.

Over the years, she had taught him so well that he became the perfect horse. He was like the last tangible trace I had left of my child's goodness, which made me feel desperate to hold on.

I collected him and moved him back to my little farm. At the time, he had a nasty cold, so I lovingly nursed him back to health and helped soothe some very raw wounds. Nightly, I buried my face in his red mane, sobbed and then wrapped my arms around his neck to inhale his scent. It felt as if I was twelve years old all over again. Sebastian withstood all of this with great patience. On many a dark night, I felt as if he was joining me in a silent prayer for his real mom's recovery.

My volume of calls/texts/emails was hectic on a normal workday, with my clients constantly in touch over their deals. Our part was critical in the closing of these multimillion-dollar commercial/industrial real estate transactions. The onslaught of life had doubled overnight with all things rehab and the unraveling of my daughter's life front and center. I needed an assistant or a nurse for Sebastian or both.

That was a nice fantasy.

Of course, I had Natasha who had bounced back to her normal, happy self. There were no signs of alcohol or strange behavior. When I had conversations with her about rehab and the dangers of being an addict, she looked at me with those baby blues and told me how she understood. "I'll never make the same mistakes as my stepsister," she assured me.

Hallelujah! I believed every syllable that Natasha told me. All I had to do was look into her eyes and see the truth.

From Deb to Marie:

Hello, my gorgeous friend. I have identified my enabling of Haley as if there was no tomorrow and it's probably because when I found the courage to leave her Mafioso father, I took her, her clothes, and mine in black trash bags. For the next six months, I lived in so much fear. I was broke with no place to live, staying on sofas, and no food sometimes.

I swore right then that no child of mine would ever go through the pain I was going through! Hahaha! Here endeth my sharing. Funny, but we are all sisters born through our courage and love for our child/children :)

Love Deb.

From Marie to Deb:

Dear Deb,

It is so amazing... sharing your heart with a friend can exhume such basic truths and bring them up to the light where we can put them to work. When you get to the point when you are actually interacting with Haley again, you will need this truth present in your mind at every turn:

Haley will never recover unless YOU are strong enough to back out and let her experience her very own pain, feel the pain, know the pain, and finally make her own choice to take on responsibility for her own life. That pain is her ticket to a new life. You are already doing this in the most courageous way I have ever seen! You are already strong enough to do this, so all you have to do is stick to it and keep going.

Remember, you were my earth angel first...

Love,
Marie

From Deb to Marie:

I am here arguing with my hubby and getting sooooo upset that he won't let me have the dogs. I told him he is only in front by a very narrow margin! I am going to check out a few places tomorrow [regarding her horse, Sebastian] that are closer to the rehab and just a little more $$, so she will be able to see him. You are my earth angel... hahaha, song title about that right, so carry right on sparkling. We all need you so much :)

From Marie to Deb:

P.S. Stop with the dogs! It's not part of the plan for them to be there for Haley to come home to after! We need to get pictures tomorrow a.m. for Saul, and my friend Jody who has a big Rottie network! We will find them someone to love them up one side and down the other... you will see! You do NOT want those dogs because Haley will come back after them. You are cutting those ties.... remember? Painful, yes... absolutely, but we will find them such a wonderful loving home! I know it! Keep the faith. They are amazing and loving and they deserve it sooo much... we will do this... I will ask my husband if they can come stay here until they find a new home... I love those big puppers! I don't know what he'll say, but let's try a ranch visit before he gets home!

Marie
Xoxo

From Deb to Eileen, (who is a British woman, a brilliant scientist and also accomplished horsewoman)

Hello my lovely friend,

It has been hell on earth this past week. I am having the hardest times letting go of Haley's dogs. A lady came to look yesterday, but she was very old and frail. Not a good match. Both the dogs just about climbed in my lap and covered me in kisses. I sobbed my heart out. I am going to take pictures of them today, so I hope that will help to place them. Her four older horses have gone up north; I donated them to a ranch for underprivileged children. Sebastian is going out to pasture, I will call around today; don't want him too far away or where it gets too cold at night. That just leaves the two ponies... I was made an offer for both of them yesterday, but the lady would keep them at the ranch they are at now- not a good idea, I think. Haley would make a B-line for that ranch the moment she can drive again.

Haley's counselor is named Butch. How perfect is his name for fighting with a demon? He said yesterday was her best day so far. She joined in a softball game and asked him to give me a very, very long list of items she needs over there, hallelujah! I am writing a daily journal, so one day Haley can read and see that I, along with my friends, also went through a lot of pain and struggled with the addiction :) :)

From Eileen to Deb:

So glad to hear Haley is on her way to recovery. It will be a long journey, but it's wonderful she has started it. Glad to hear you found a home for the horses. I hope they adjust to their new lives better than we do. When I adopted Delilah, my neighbor's Great Dane, I was amazed that almost immediately she was part of our gang.
Lots of blessings blowing your way.

Love,
Eileen

From Deb to Rachel

Hey My Honey,
I have to wash all Haley's clothes this morning and then pack her a couple of suitcases. My stepson is coming over this afternoon to be the taxi service and run them over there. Yesterday was sooooo painful for me. Jake thinks that somehow, I associate the dogs with giving away the last part of my daughter; I just want a good home for them. I will go and take pictures this afternoon. I am starting a daily journal; wish I could stop crying. Sometimes I feel like I have a host of avenging angels helping me to stay strong and battle the demon in my daughter. I have angels in human form -- kind, compassionate and strong. Then sometimes I am just a sobbing mess! Perhaps with my journal, my daughter will see she was not the only one on a painful journey.

From Rachel to Deb:

That is true about your journal. It is good for you and later may be of help for Haley. Addicts not only inflict pain and suffering on themselves, but those they have in their care, and those who care for them. You know no matter how many times in this ordeal she says she hates you, or she is done with you, or screams, or whatever... the bottom line is she loves you and wants love from you and others. She just has to relearn to love herself and love herself enough to work hard and get out of this dismal abyss she got sucked into by her wrong choices.

I know the dogs are actually the hardest things because we love our dogs like children and they are so loving unconditionally. We know how much Haley loves her dogs and other animals, so you feel bad for her and bad for the dogs. But I guess for now, it just has to be and we will not stop until we find them a good and loving home like we did the piggies and the bunny, as well as the cat.

This whole event and the years of stress that led up to it will, of course, totally strain your relationship with Jake. He cannot possibly understand or handle all that you must be going through this time. Now, of all times, you need to be supported and remain advocates for each other. He needs to be your gentle rock, as you have no doubt have been his in the past. You must, in a safe place, tell him what you need from him: love, kindness, understanding, and support, etc. Cry all you need to cry. It's not good to hold things in, and you've been so strong through this and accomplished so much. You must let it out, so you can continue to be strong and get through all you need to and heal yourself as well as watch your daughter.

I am a sensitive person. I have only known you and Haley for a short time, but going through this with you as your friend has been a lot for me as a person. I cannot even imagine what it is like for you as a mother who loves her daughter and worries about her and her animals.

Remember, Marie and I are always here for you if you need a shoulder to cry on or a hand to hold, or words to hear, or just someone to sit quietly with you.

You are a special person and we love you.

Rachel
xoxo

One night, I received a phone call from a nice chap I knew from work. Coincidentally, he saw the posters of the dogs and wanted to come by with his wife to meet them. It was a tough day in many ways including a doctor's appointment for Natasha and then a meeting with the school board about her future or lack of one. We made it to the shelter in the nick of time to spring the dogs.

Bono and Maverick were overjoyed to see us and I loved how they jumped so high to kiss us to death. All Bono wanted was his rubs. The entire shelter broke my heart. The dog next door to ours had his life story pinned to his cage door. It read: "Please take me home. I am seven years old and my friend and I have always lived together. My friend just got adopted, but they did not take me. And our Dad just died."

Oh, that still brings huge body racking sobs from me. If only I could rescue all four and two legged beings and take away their pain and fear.

That night all we could do is spring our two boys from the shelter and take them back home to meet their potential new parents. I watched as our two beautiful and huge dogs flew around the garden, my heart delighting in watching them run out of sheer happiness. I let my own smaller size herd of dogs out to play, feeling like the Pied

Piper as they all followed me around.

The prospective parents soon arrived, and they loved the size of the big dogs. I learned that they lived on a small farm that was an acre.

Yes, both dogs would be welcome to sleep in bed with them.

And so, it was done. I was both happy and simultaneously suicidal as I gave away my only grandchildren besides Sebastian.

The evening ended the only way it could with me screaming at Jake and sobbing on the bed.

I had regressed to my seven-year-old self.

Note from new dog owners-

Subj: You Rock.

They slept like babies last night in our room. Our family is in love with them! Thanks again!

From Rachel to Deb:

Hi Deb!

I just came home and got Marie's wonderful message that the boys had found a good home! I'm so happy for them and you and so greatly relieved. I think about them all the time. I even just asked a new person this morning if they would take them to no avail. Please thank the new dog parents for me, too. They deserved a good home together. I could just cry with happiness for them.

Rachel

CHAPTER
TEN

TOUGH LOVE

I t was time to use my newly acquired tough love muscle. I only felt empowered to flex it because of Butch who was Haley's counselor in rehab and with whom I spoke daily about her progress. Butch didn't want to shield her from life and insisted we set up a call where I would tell her about her animals. Knowing this would be deeply emotional, Marie offered to come sit with me and basically hold my hand knowing I would get the brunt of Haley's rage. I even wrote out a speech and rehearsed it with Marie playing the role of my daughter.

On the scheduled day, my heart was pounding, and I felt as if I wanted to throw up my breakfast. I decided to tell Haley the brutal facts of life. "When you're an unfit mother, your children have to be taken away and placed in caring homes. I know you loved all of your animals, but you're sick and not in a position to care for them any longer," I told her.

Tough love at its finest.

Butch later told me that the blood curdling screams that left

Haley's lungs echoed throughout the entire hospital. I may as well have driven a stake through her heart. Just knowing that left me running to the bathroom to actually throw up.

There was also the task of visiting my daughter at a rehab. Family time was at 7 p.m. each night and I had a very long drive, so I had to crawl through rush hour to get to her. Early on, Jake had decided that he would forgo these family meetings, so I went on my own.

The process at rehab included guests leaving our bags at the reception desk where a steely-eyed lady checked the visitors in. I was told that Haley was outside in the smoking area. Opening the door, I was always engulfed in a thick fog of smoke that seemed to permanently linger in the air. It took a moment for the air to clear for me to actually spot her face. One night, I noticed that she had put on weight and it looked good on her.

She saw me, smiled and then burst into a torrent of awful words, blaming me with searing anger for the loss of her animals. After that purge, Haley turned the torrent off like flipping a switch. She shifted back to being a loving child who decided to hug me, sob on my neck and even hold my hand.

Oh, how I wanted to wrap her in a big safety blanket of love.

We also sat side-by-side in the family meeting hall with others who shared this precious time. I told the group, "I'm so grateful that my daughter is in the program." The truth is I could have kissed everyone there.

She was on an emotional rollercoaster, bouncing back and forth between rage and neediness. By the time I left rehab, I was emotionally spent with a three-hour drive ahead of me. Then the storm hit. How perfect! Tears were rolling down my face as Mother Nature poured out her own heart.

How did we get here?

The night played out in my mind like a movie I kept rewinding. At one point, I wasn't paying attention to my driving. In a terrifying moment, I noticed that I couldn't see anything anymore thanks to the hard rain.

I mentally slapped myself.

"For God's sake, pull yourself together, Deb!" I shouted.

Where was that tough love now?

I knew that a quick call to Jake would make me feel better.

"I feel you're really getting into this Deb," he chided me when it came to rehab and my daughter. "And, by the way, I would really appreciate a home cooked dinner one night soon."

Wow.

I felt so incredibly alone and unable to do anything well. I was a bad wife now – as well as being a bad mother. My deepest wish was for Jake to show me some compassion and kindness. All I knew is that I failed to get a hot dinner on the table just as I had failed to give my daughter a happy life.

I was a failure.

How could my husband be so unmoved? No matter how fast my tap dance, no one was entertained in our house, least of all me. I felt hopeless, inadequate and miserable. I even told Marie that I thought I was showing some resemblance to the Stockholm syndrome.

I kept most of my sorrows locked in different boxes with the lids tightly closed and duct-taped for good measure. From an early age, I knew how not to give authenticity to any negative feelings I might be experiencing.

Stuff it down. Apologize. Start over. It must always be my fault.

I was terrified of what still lurked in those boxes, so I left them sealed. There was no time to wallow, because my girls needed me.

I kept that stiff upper lip and decided to carry on without

complaint. The loop played in my mind: Put others first and don't be a burden. Be cheerful! Once again, I stuffed the rising emotions back down my throat with the heel of my biggest boot.

I remembered my stepfather's words: "I need to break your spirit. You're way too willful."

I wondered if indeed my will had been broken now. If it was just gone temporarily, I prayed that someone would please return it to me.

Was I a bad person? I decided that I was one. Maybe if I had tap-danced faster then everything would have been okay.

As I drove down those torturous rain drenched highways on my way home from rehab to make that home cooked dinner, my tears flowed in pace with the weather. For once, I allowed my heart to burst and my sadness box to open.

I sent the following emails to my intervention angels:

I saw Haley yesterday, she has been in for just over three weeks.

I was just expecting to discuss her progress with her wonderful counselor Butch, plus I wanted to go over the finances of her stay. When Butch invited Haley to join us, he had already gone over the plan with her.

Haley will be entering sober living on the 30th day of rehab (next week).

Haley was going to sign a contract agreeing to voluntarily commit herself back to intensive 90-day rehab if for any reason Butch sees her drug test results as less than they should be. Also, there will be no visits from Mom during that 90-day period.

Haley has agreed to stay in sober living for nine months. It is luckily only a couple of blocks away from the hospital which will allow her to participate in a full schedule of outpatient programs and continue to see Butch.

Haley understands that less than ten percent succeed in staying drug free, but she sounds really determined.

I took her for lunch and was a bit nervous. I had to tell her I had disposed of all of her worldly possessions and most of her clothes. She actually handled the news really well and said she was glad Christmas was almost here. Maybe then I could get her some new larger clothes. She said "stuff" did not bother her, but the loss of her animals did.

Haley also teased Butch and said that the reason he was sad was that she would no longer be a live-in patient and he would miss her on the softball team. :)

I wrote in my diary the following: My daughter actually appeared for lunch yesterday and it was wonderful to see her again. She was funny, kind, sad, yet determined.

Please keep praying for her. Recovery is about baby steps, but I am overjoyed those steps are going in the right direction.

Deb

CHAPTER ELEVEN

THE BEST MADE PLANS

Haley was supposed to be in rehab for 30 days and then move to the sober home for nine months. I could finally breathe because we had a solid plan of action. It was only a few days away from her 30-day graduation, and I was excited because this was a major milestone.

The phone rang. It was the 29th day.

On the other end was a very irate man from the rehab center. I couldn't believe what he was telling me. "Haley has gone AMA," he said in a hurried voice. My mind scrambled to figure it out as I asked him, "What is AMA?" I missed the rest of his words as he tried to explain this secret rehab code that I was supposed to understand.

His personal volume got louder, but this didn't improve my learning curve or hearing. He shouted the words again: "AMA stands for Against Medical Advice!" he ranted. "Your daughter has left the rehab against the advice of her doctors."

It sounded like a scene from the movie *Thelma and Louise*.

Despite the best-made plans, Haley left rehab the old-fashioned way by running up the road as the nurses were chasing her.

My brain practically imploded. "She what?" I cried.

Somewhere deep in my mind, I hoped that he was describing the wrong patient. He went on to explain to me that this move would preclude her from having medical insurance cover her for the outpatient part of the program.

Oh, dear God!

All I could think of was my last credit card, which was exhausted. How would I pay the medical bills now? How could she be so irresponsible and do this to me? That same man on the other end of the bad news hotline explained to me that Haley left with another young lady who had been medically released. Haley felt the need to go with her new friend in order to "protect her from her abusive husband."

There was nothing they could do to stop her.

One question remained: Where the heck was my daughter? I spent a frantic 72 hours wondering where the hell she was living and if she was doing drugs? Was she splayed on a street corner dead? With each passing hour, I could literally feel myself growing older as something deep inside began to crumble out of fear.

Jake wanted to get my mind off it, and we went out for a bite to eat. It was odd that our neighbor called me while we were out. When I rang him back, I was informed that he heard loud, whooping screams of delight on our property. I knew it was Haley. She must have scaled our gate and spotted both her truck and the horse I told her were gone.

My credibility was a little wobbly.

But my mothering instincts were solid. There was joy in knowing that my child was still alive.

Haley wasn't waiting for us calmly on the living room couch. She was still gone and another 24 hours passed with no news. Another neighbor rang me again a few days later. It was 7 a.m. She just wanted to pass along the news that a strange truck was parked outside our gate. Tossing on my robe, I trudged down the steep hill to our front gate on an absolutely freezing November morning.

I couldn't clearly see inside the car parked on the other side of our gate because the windows were almost 100 percent fogged.

When I called out, two frozen girls climbed out of the car looking brittle, blue and so very vulnerable.

I knew Jake would surely go over the edge when he heard about our new arrivals. Apparently, Haley and her girlfriend had slept outside in the freezing, bitter cold. My daughter was nervous as she stood there gauging my reaction. Even I was nervous as my reaction formed.

"Mom, we have a great sober living half-way house to move into right now," Haley informed me.

"I'd like to go and look for myself," I replied.

Stay calm, I told myself. Resist all urges to strangle her.

They were still somewhat on the plan...

And most importantly, she was willingly going to the next sobriety step. I reminded myself that life is what happens when you are making other plans.

At least, there was a plan, right?

Both girls did move into that new sober living facility. Haley even had a new cell phone again and was using it to give me progress reports. "Mom, I have to walk two blocks every morning to get my Adderall medicine and this neighborhood is not safe," she said. Old habits were suddenly clicking back into place. My enabling behavior returned as I shot off a quick Email to the owner of the halfway house asking if Haley could have her medicine kept in his sober house. The same day, her counselor Butch called and my sanity returned. I fired off another Email saying to the sober living owner to please ignore my first email.

"The walk will do her good," I wrote.

It wasn't long before Thanksgiving rolled around, and Haley came home for the first time. I woke early on that holiday morning to feed and clean my horses. My daughter arrived and wandered to the stables to help me. She was so genuinely caring and truly helpful that it felt like old times. She even told funny jokes as she helped me clean.

When I looked back, I saw her in the same position I had been in on many nights. Her arms were wrapped around Sebastian's neck and she began to sob.

I knew she missed him. I could feel her pain. Oh, how I wished I had a wand in that moment to heal her in one sweep of my magic fairy dusty. I wanted to end this nightmare with one tiny spell.

Without that wand, I allowed Haley to cry and even gave her space to do it. Later, it was just Haley, Jake and I for Thanksgiving dinner. I decided we would eat at a local café to make it less weird for all of us. The conversation between bites was a little bit stilted. Jake was surprised when Haley announced she didn't want to eat her dinner because she "needed to go on a diet." She had actually gained a few pounds and was embarrassed by her extra weight. "Oh, Haley," I said. "Your face looks so healthy and beautiful now." She didn't seem convinced.

In that moment, I knew her sobriety was as fragile as a leaf blowing in those cold fall winds.

Jake and I ate and then allowed Haley to drive us home. Jake even teased her about her heavy driving foot as we whooshed over Malibu Canyon.

It was a pleasant night and Haley spent the night but woke up cranky. Her new theme song became several choruses of "I need my car back."

"Please, I really need my car back."

"Give me back my frickin' car..........please."

"Where are my car keys?"

Hindsight being 20-20, (and I learn better backwards), I would have sold that bloody car a long time ago, so she wouldn't have even seen it sitting there.

She also wanted to get her nails and toes done. So, I dropped her off at a salon because I hated seeing them looking so unkempt. Win-win for me, and I was handed a couple of hours break from her while I got to look at a not-so-ragged daughter.

Back at the house, it was close to dinner time and Haley began to scream at me about the car. Jake was the only one who was happy. "This dinner tastes really good," he told me. At least, someone was happy.

All of a sudden, Haley was a case study in all things miserable. She just wouldn't let up on all the reasons why she needed that car back now and a few of her arguments made sense to me. She did need to go to A.A. meetings on a regular basis. I just wished she would stop talking, but her verbal tirade was unrelenting.

"Mom," she posed, switching tactics. "Can I just borrow your car? I want to see my boyfriend for just an hour."

Alarms bells clanged in my mind. Her boyfriend was still a heroin addict and user, as far as I knew.

"I just want to get laid," Haley informed us.

"I'll buy you a vibrator," I offered.

It was a much-needed laugh to break up all the tension.

Haley went to bed that night absolutely disgusted with us while I felt sorry for Jake. Perhaps it was too soon for her to be home for three consecutive nights when just one would have been perfect.

The next morning, I was scheduled to take her back to her sober living home, and frankly, couldn't wait to drop her off. After weeks of non-stop stress, I couldn't bear to go another round. On the way to her new home, I stopped to buy her new jeans in a larger size, which she found funny. We even swung by the horse barn close to her sober living residence.

I wrote a check I couldn't afford to put Sebastian there, which was closer to her. I knew he would be her best therapy and Butch agreed. God knows, I wanted her to get well. I even suggested that she bring other patients out to the barn to help groom him.

One more stop. Haley had a brand-new blender, so she could make healthy shakes for breakfast.

Small steps, but they were important.

The next day, I rounded up my wonderful Marie who was going to help me deliver Sebastian to Haley. Up since six a.m., I was busy packing the horse stuff and figured I had to make a quick run to Costco to buy a bicycle for Haley. It's the best way for her to make the ten-mile round trip to the stables. I had to smile because her new lifestyle kept getting healthier and healthier.

We arrived with Sebastian and I was delighted at the manicured lawns by this new stable. I was also worried and hoped they didn't add a lot of extras to the monthly bill. The box stall reminded me of tiny cages. Poor Sebastian. One ray of light was directed my way when the manager said a pipe corral would be available on December 1.

"Done," I told him, reiterating that we didn't need any extra services.

One of Haley's new sober living friends drove her over and he seemed to be a nice chap. "I'm so glad you survived the recent fire," he told me.

I was so stressed that even a mushroom shaped cloud and local fire with bursts that went off like atom bombs over the horizon of my house didn't make much of an impression or dent in my day. Over 30 nearby homes were burned to the ground. I allowed myself to feel sorrow and compassion for those families.

I chatted with the nice chap some more and learned that he was a professor at Pepperdine University in Malibu for sixteen years before addiction turned his life upside down. What a waste, I thought, but then remembered that addiction is an equal opportunity caller.

Haley took one look at her new bike and was dumbstruck. Quickly, she let me know she would not be riding it. The Pepperdine professor offered to put it in his van, so she could have it back at the sober house. Overwhelmed and prickly, she obviously wanted us to leave. Marie was the one who reminded me that I couldn't unpack everything or settle her in. "Deb, she can do that for herself," she said.

It was so hard for me to drive away and leave her with her horse stuff all over the ground. I was truly glad that her boy, Sebastian, was with her and hoped that he would bring her solace and remind her to stay strong.

CHAPTER TWELVE

SOBER HOUSE

My first visit to her sober house left me totally appalled. It looked like some kind of frat house and the thick wall of black cigarette smoke made me gag. There were people of all different ages and genders just lying around, smoking and watching television.

This is not what I expected. How could anyone stay sober under these conditions? They must have been bored to tears.

This inspired me to write a letter to the owner of the house:

Hello There Barry:

I hope you had a wonderful Thanksgiving. Here are my thoughts as I have taken the liberty of writing down how I would like to see my daughter helped. I had mistakenly thought that when the rehab center said they reintegrate patients into society, there would be more tangible help with baby steps toward self-reliance. I have learned that whatever age the addict starts using is where they are mentally, plus Haley was always young and naïve for her age. Around 18/19 is where she is now.

My daughter has been sick for so many years. She will need a lot of "steps." I know the addict has to want their recovery, but I also think the reason the relapse rate is so high may be due to the lack of structure once they enter sober living.

I just feel there must be more steps and structure in place so that success is absolutely an option for those that might falter. Haley loves your house, so please don't take any of this in a way that would be hurtful.

I am just going to write these in no particular order of importance:

*I would love for the female manager to help Haley with being aware if her nails are filthy (I seem to have a thing with that). I would like her to go from being an unaware drug addict to taking pride in how she looks in order to become an aware, functioning and autonomous adult.

*I would like her to hand in her cell phone at 11 p.m. and have it returned in the morning.

*I would like all patients to be woken up at a reasonable time.

*For the first 90 days, there should be a logbook that she signs to go in and out of the house. She should list where she is going, whom she is with, as well as her return time. Actually, I would love if one of the senior patients could go with her, in the AA spirit of service, to help a newbie stay clean.

*Haley does not yet have a sponsor. She has mentioned to me

that some people succeed on their own. A very bad idea. I would like to know Haley has the staff's cell phone numbers programmed into hers, or again, a senior patient with her, so that when she has a meltdown then she will instantly know whom to call or ask for help.

*Maybe some of this already happens at the house and Haley has just not told me, but I thought it would be good to read from the AA book each morning in a group, and then to meditate for serenity and strength in the coming day.

*On Saturdays and Sundays, at a set time, I'd like her to receive guidance and help in managing her time (with ADHD being one of her biggest challenges) for the coming week. She should write out the days of the week and account for all her waking hours.

*I would love to see the girls coming off meth to be taught good food habits including how to cook healthy meals and how to plan their grocery list and budget, as weight issues seem to be a trigger.

*Can you provide a list of local therapists who specialize in addiction and also anger management?

*She will need help with putting resume together in order to get a part-time job.

*There should be weekly group viewings of local employment opportunities and help with how to apply.

*I'd like her to be taught basic life skills including how to

balance a checkbook, how to take baby steps with aspirations and how to get from point A to point B. The chasm between A and B seems overwhelmingly large for her at the moment.

*I would like to see weekly mandatory volunteering for the less fortunate -- AIDS patients, the children's ward, Meals on Wheels, soup kitchens, etc. I would say the animal shelter, but Haley would want to adopt all of the inmates. I am sure there are many worthy causes in your area that would love extra sets of hands.

*Many of the girls coming off of crystal meth, like Haley, put on a ton of weight. She must have put on thirty pounds. When she was here visiting, she had already started to fixate on her weight, which of course, would be a trigger. I think it is essential that they are encouraged to go kickboxing or to the gym. For those that have lost their driving privileges, or for whatever reasons do not have a car with them, an arrangement can be made with a local shuttle or taxi service, for a fixed rate for the girls. Nowhere is farther than five miles, and Haley told me she and her girlfriend paid $25 for a one-way trip back from the gym, which they can't afford and is extortion. If you could maybe negotiate with a local company an affordable price, it would be wonderful. This way, the girls can get safely around and attend classes at night. Maybe the senior patients that have cars could be of service on different days of the week? Maybe those without cars could pay $20 for a round trip. The round trip could be at a set time, so that the "helper" is not run ragged.

*I have moved Haley's horse to Pasadena, as Butch said this would be wonderful therapy. She can be of service to the other

patients, as she can share the care and grooming of her horse with them.

*Haley is waging an unrelenting "war" against me for her car to be returned to her. When she was home with me, she was going nuts wanting to visit her old boyfriend. Of course, a car is not a good idea for her in the foreseeable future. I am concerned that at night, it's dangerous in your neighborhood, so her bicycle is out of the question past dark.

I am fully expecting Haley to be in sober living for nine months. I have heard the longer she stays, the greater her chances are of being clean. I feel a busy, scheduled person is a happy person. Idle hands do the devil's work.

My saying for myself: "The road to hell is paved with good intentions."

All the best,
Deb

Phew! I'm exhausted just reading through the list now. It's funny, but Barry actually sent me a lovely reply saying that many changes were actually on the way and would start in January. I felt a giddy mix of relief and hope.

If only my daughter didn't have "other" plans. Her new instant best girlfriend was leaving this sober house. This was the same girl Haley had discharged herself with from rehab and later followed to this place. Apparently, the rent was being raised and Haley had heard through the grapevine that it was something to do with a letter I sent offering suggestions.

My daughter was royally pissed off at me. She told me the only way she would continue in sober living is if she could move with her new best friend to another sober home down the road. Apparently, there were many of these places in the area and none that were controlled by any government agency. Even I could open up a sober living facility with all of my several weeks of experience under my belt! It struck me as so bizarre that such an important place wasn't regulated or monitored.

This would not become my hill to die on. In the end, Haley moved to the next frat house where she was promptly kicked out the day after Christmas – along with her bestie – for violating a rule.

The rule was that you couldn't "fraternize" with patients of the opposite sex.

Here we would go …again.

And so, Haley moved home with us. On the first night, I remember giving her a pair of really pretty, white PJs to wear.

"Do you like them, darling?" I asked.

She gave me a sheepish smile. "They're a bit institutional, Mom."

I had to laugh. I was shocked those muscles still worked.

As we settled into our new lives with Haley at home, I extolled the benefits of healthy living including quitting smoking.

"Whoa! Easy, Mom," she said, "I've just given up drugs." Her huge smile, the one that melted my heart, brought another laugh-out-loud moment.

Maybe, somehow, we would come out of this on the other side.

There were other matters that required my attention. I was upside down financially when it came to her truck. I had just arrived home from working in Texas and was leaving for New York that afternoon on business. When we got the truck, I literally ran into the car dealership and signed the papers. Haley had negotiated terms. It must have gone along the lines of how much money can we pay you for this truck. Now in the present time I still owed more on it than it was worth. I couldn't even give it away.

My stupidity had me in this pickle.

A word about our home: It was way out in the countryside. Buses didn't stop there, and cabs were expensive.

Of course, I gave her the truck back.

Really?

Yes, really.

From Marie to Deb:

I am afraid that Haley is being set-up to fail by having free reign to go wherever she wants, especially at night, when everyone is partying. I know she has good intentions and I know she's an adult, but the addiction was so very much more powerful than she. I wish you could somehow find a very structured environment and structured schedule with full accountability for her whereabouts all day and night for at least a year or so where she could blossom into her purpose.

I just don't think such a long-term problem can poof be gone forever unless there is a very, very solid structure built around her. She already told us the other night that her friends at the sober living have fallen back at some point. I don't know if that was for dramatic effect or not? But, it sounds logical to me.

It would only take one weak moment for her to be right back at ground zero, and it seems risky for her to be around others who are partying. What are the people she's out with doing at all hours of the night if not partying? She is still very attracted to musicians and that whole world. She was talking about being out late at bars the other night, which is something that just doesn't seem to lead to success.

I remember hearing many, many times that one of the most important parts of recovery is keeping the right company at all times. I don't think that company is found at bars, with musicians, and driving around late at night.

It just seems like there needs to be something more for her long-term success. It would feel better if there was more support around your angel in order to help keep her sparkling bright. She is truly soooo beautiful!

I know your gut has been telling you the same all along. If you keep looking and putting it out there to the Universe, I think the right answer will present itself. Meanwhile, fingers crossed and positive thoughts for the time being.

I'll call you later.
Xoxo,
Marie

Dec 31st. New Year's Eve.

The following is another letter/email I wrote to the owner of the sober living house. Poor chap, and I apologize in advance for repeating myself:

Barry, Happy Almost New Year!

It has been a rollercoaster here for me with Haley home. Initially, the humble, happy, bright young lady that came to stay was soooo wonderful to be around. I am so hopeful that girl wins out against her demons and stays all the time. God has blessed me with earth angels. My next-door neighbor was an addict. She is now fifteen years sober, and was one of my close friends even before she moved next door. She gives me hope.

Things have not been sitting well with me for the last few days. There's a big knot in my tummy, and I know my neighbor has no hidden agenda, so I really value her guidance.

Haley has been staying here over the holidays. I'm learning there is a name for everything. She calls this her "pink period." She has been proclaiming that she is drug free and all should be well with the world.

It turns out I am the master enabler where Haley is concerned. For starters, she has her car back. Of course, I justify that because I wanted to keep her safe at night (I am so glad you are now offering transportation). The downside is that she has been free to go …anywhere.

I had her tested and she is clean. However, I told my neighbor the following and she said, "Yep, she's clean, but she still has a long way to go."

Haley has been playing this virtual horse game where you breed horses and enter shows. At first, it looks harmless enough; however, she can be online for hours and hours at a time. When I was out shopping, I noticed my credit card was missing. Upon returning home, I asked Haley and she admitted to "borrowing" it, gave it back to me and I canceled it. She had run up $300 on the game with endless $15 entry fees. All my credit cards are totally maxed out from my own insanity of *trying to keep her afloat (enabler extraordinaire).*

I had given all my kids AAA cards to keep them safe. Haley went through her four call outs and I received a bill for over $200.

She has been breezing into rooms, a huge smile on her pretty face, telling me now that she is sober she is going to find a home, get a job and live a normal life. I hope this doesn't include Mom paying the rent, her boyfriend moving in or any slips in her sobriety. Off we go again.

Haley did interview for a job at the Equestrian Center in Burbank and if she were to get the job, I wonder if she will be able to get a ride back and forth each day? Of course, she could pay for that part of it from her salary.

My neighbor helped me to come up with my power points. I am willing to support her sobriety, pay for her stay at the sober house, plus vocational trade school efforts, gym, plus her horse for six more months. Haley would be required to pay for cigs, games, clothes, beauty, entertainment and gasoline.

Here are my terms:

*Haley needs to get a sponsor of the same sex that has been ten years sober and talk to that person every day. She needs a job and to save, so that eventually she can move into a shared situation with her own room, but on her dime with no help anymore from Mom.
*She has Wellbutrin to take every day and frankly, it helps her so much. Someone should make sure she takes it each morning. Dr. T has over-prescribed her ADD medication, so maybe we need to get her tested again for ADD to find out what the dosage should be. I think it's way too high. Haley should not take it after 1 p.m. or she will never sleep. She is enrolled in the

RC outpatient program; maybe one of their doctors could call Dr. Taylor and ask her to half the dosage.

I think the way that Haley can help others is once she is on good ground, she can then drive others back and forth. Haley can take the other patients out to her horse where they can help groom him. He would love that attention. Perhaps the other patients can help Haley with her reading skills. She also needs to learn how to prepare healthy food, as she lives on McDonalds take-out.

Haley says she wants to still pursue her acting. I agree that she is talented, but that career is such a crapshoot and creates really bad self-esteem if you are not a size zero.

I really think Haley will flourish in a structured, loving, family unit away from me for a while. Jake and I agree we will not have her home for more than one night until she is a year sober.

If Haley chooses to break any rules, she may not come home. If she chooses not to go to Marengo House, she may not come home. However, the car will return depending on how you advise me. She will be totally on her own and penniless.

She's clean now, but I fully understand we all have a long way to go.

I would like her to return to you on Jan 3.. I'm going to ask Butch if I can tell her all of this in his office on that day. My neighbor told me not to discuss it with her here at my home, but to act like everything is normal.

I would like to go with the fully supervised program for the first month, even though I am stretched beyond thin. I want her recovery more than anything else in the whole world. Sorry to go on so.

P.S. Would love to see her volunteering somewhere: AIDS,

food kitchen......something.

Happy New Year!
Big hug
Deb.

Talk about being repetitive in my desires.

I reached out for help to Pat the interventionist.

Hi there Pat :)

I hope you had a wonderful New Year. I have been busy learning about all the things I have no knowledge of concerning recovery. Where to start?

I filled her in on what happened next including the new revelation that Haley wasn't attending her outpatient program. And then I wrote:

Now, Haley wants money. She tells me, "Oh, I am fine Mom. I have wasted enough time and I need to get going. How can you punish me now that I am clean? You helped me so much before. It would just be a little loan."

My husband is so biased against Haley. I can't chat with him over my concerns. All he does is walk around and ask when she is leaving. I told my neighbor, fifteen years sober, of her behavior since she has been home including late, late nights and seeing the old boyfriend who first told me she was using. Now, she wants to help him get clean. I feel sick in my stomach again as I write this and see my glaring mistakes. She's playing the online horse game for hours and hours, "borrowing" my credit card without permission and sleeping until late in the day.

I feel she's over exuberant in her proclamations of sobriety. She doesn't even have a sponsor.

My neighbor listened and reminded me that Haley may be sober, but she is far from cured. She advised me to have a "mini" intervention again. I met with John yesterday and he advised me that Haley should go into a solid 90-day program.

Even though the sober house is offering the structure she needs now, we don't want her to be the beta test. He suggested Milestone Ranch. Marie visited there late yesterday for me and they give scholarships to worthy patients. There is also the Women's Program in Santa Barbara. John feels a good, solid 90 days and then a structured sober living arrangement are the building blocks missing. She really is at about 18-years-old mentally and a young 18 at that.

Haley has announced that she is finding her own home. She also told us that she's lonely without a dog. Late last night, she came home with a puppy. I was asleep in bed while Haley and Jake got into it badly. He wants her OUT even if she has to stay at a motel or hotel. I hope she returned the puppy, but her truck is here. She's sleeping and I'm allowing her to do so as I get my ducks in a row.

I feel as if the bottom has dropped out of my plan again.

I can't deal with Haley directly. I don't even know what's appropriate now, which is why I'm reaching out. I feel myself returning to my old, enabling ways, which won't help Haley succeed to flap her wings. I'm just a pushover where she's concerned.

Please, would you retake me on as a client, follow along every step of the way on Haley's progress, and send me the email updates? Once the huge hurdle is crossed off and we get her back to a place, I know she'll be guided in the right *direction again.*

Greg from Milestones told Marie that meth addicts damage the front part of their brain, which disables the ability to think beyond today or be concerned with the consequences of actions. The puppy is a good example.

Haley will admit she is an addict now. She is in her "pink" phase. I am truly blessed to have such wonderful, compassionate friends; I wish I had done a better job. Please let me know your thoughts on how to proceed.

There really is an incredibly talented, kind young lady in there. She has such a sparkle and compassion for others. Please help me to save her.

Respectfully Yours.
Deb

From John
To Deb, Pat, and Marie:

Ladies:

Good morning Deb... well written, with the exception of two things: one, you have done a good job with the tools you had at the time. You are now gaining new tools to deal with all of this stuff differently. Do not beat yourself up... that is a directive, okay? Secondly, and I believe Pat will agree with me, there is NO CURE for Haley. There is only recovery-- one day at a time. The recovery process is life-long, and all parties need to be motivated to take on that philosophy.

I spoke with Pat yesterday after I had lunch with you and Marie. So, she had a head's up and is checking on a few things already per our discussion.

Pat... please let me know what else I can be doing to

support the process, including talking with Denise and/or Glen about the possibility of Haley obtaining a scholarship into Milestones… if you think that is a good clinical option for her long-term healing and recovery.

I am planning to be up in the Santa Barbara area soon and would like to do a site visit myself of Casa Serena. I would like to get to know the staff and program better, especially based on our discussion yesterday. Please share with me what you can about the program once you revisit it.

Happy New Year.

Best regards,
John

The "pink" period describes how an addict lives his or her life after recently getting sober. I wished I was in my pink period.

Instead, my mood was dark when I found out that Haley was given an abandoned dog, a Doberman, which didn't bother me. Jake however was scared to death of the breed. Haley later would admit that she knew Jake felt this way and that would make it impossible for the dog, (and Haley), to stay at home with us.

The fun continued when she moved in with her old boyfriend who thus became her current man. He was living with his parents and I was so grateful that they allowed her to move in. Her boyfriend's Mom was a lovely woman, but I knew she would have zero control over my daughter. At least she had a safe, although temporary, roof over her head, even if it meant being with this boyfriend who supposedly wasn't using anymore.

Not that she would lie to me.

CHAPTER THIRTEEN

MUSTANG SALLY

January arrived with a fresh blast of cold winter air. We barely noticed the adverse weather, or world events for that matter, as this coincided with the simultaneous unraveling of my daughters' lives. Yes, this was the new Bizarro Land that Jake and I suddenly inhabited together. It was something you never wanted to have in common with your mate.

Lovely Natasha did not drive until she was seventeen because we wanted her to wait and mature for another year, thus making her a more responsible driver. During that January of Haley's brief return to live at home, we purchased Natasha her first car.

It was a used, white Mustang that was gorgeous. Natasha researched cars online and felt as if she had found the best price. She even negotiated with the salesperson and showed us her data to back up her find. All in all: quite mature. I was impressed with her focus and persuasion skills because soon she had both Jake and I sitting at a local dealership signing on the dotted line.

Correction: I signed.

The girl had four parents and I was the one signing. After the paperwork was complete, we had agreed to let Natasha drive by her friend's house and show off her new baby. She was thrilled and we felt the same way for her.

"Don't do anything bad, baby," Jake warned her with a kiss.

"Of course not, Dad," Natasha replied. She was slightly put out that he would issue this kind of warning. What could possibly happen?

Late that Saturday night, the phone rang and I nearly jumped out of my skin. Jake answered and immediately went a ghastly shade of pale.

"Deb," he said in a rush, "Natasha and her boyfriend are in the hospital. An ambulance came to take the boyfriend. Natasha fell down the flight of stairs chasing after him and the paramedics."

Jake looked at me with worried eyes.

"Stay here in bed," he said. "I'll go."

For hours, I sat wide-awake in bed waiting for my husband to return while my heart did that familiar loud thumping. At 4 a.m., he came home ashen and exhausted.

"Natasha and her boyfriend are both hooked up to IVs," he said. "Alcohol poisoning."

I sat bolt upright. We were not losing another child to addiction and drugs!

I was the mother of all things rehab. That is what I believed with a real zeal.

At first, Jake agreed and we set the wheels in motion by calling Serene Life (where Natasha's best friend had stayed). A bed was available at this under-18 facility. I researched it as thoroughly as I could in those wee hours and had long phone calls with the people who would be in charge of our daughter's care.

It was Sunday morning and finally Natasha was released from

the hospital. Jake brought her home with the hangover from hell. I was so glad to see her, but I was also a Mom on a mission. Jake and I had concocted a story. "Since you're under eighteen, we received a call from child protective services. We need to meet with them – all of us – on Monday morning," Jake told her.

Natasha went to sleep, and I drove to Target to get the uniform of white T-shirts and other stuff she needed for her month stay in rehab. I ripped the tags off in the garage and quickly packed a suitcase that we stashed in my car. Meanwhile, Jake and I only exchanged notes and emails that day as Natasha always had superhuman hearing.

From Deb to Exey

Hello There Darling:

I am sorry for the bad news.

I have set up the appointment on Monday at one p.m. and we are not telling Natasha she is staying, but rather that the policeman who threatened to call child services last night has made it mandatory.

The population is made up of mainly likable, sociable, happy kids that keep making bad choices. Joy, the woman I spoke to on the phone, said that often these kids are extraordinary in some way... artists, creative people, etc. It is a dual diagnosis hospital, so she will see a psychiatrist, as well as a therapist. There will also be private therapy five times a week, twice a week family therapy and a strong spiritual bond to a higher power including meditation, relaxation and church on Sunday morning. There are also private gyms they will attend each morning, plus anger management classes and a course in the healing of the afflicted mind.

The academic portion will include attending the charter school there. An academic facilitator is on staff and will see her transcript on Monday and choose her courses. For the first seven days, they want her to disengage from the outside world, so we will not be able to talk to her; however, the counselor and doctors can call and email us. After that first week, she will be able to call us. They have a strong link with AA and attend meetings throughout the week. Her time is accounted for 24/7. Natasha will earn her privileges back. I am going to Target today to get her white t-shirts, which along with jeans are the uniform for everyone.

After the first week, the kids tend to thrive and do well. I will email you daily and call you tomorrow or Monday.

At the facility, Natasha appeared from her bedroom for long enough to inform us all that she did not think she had done anything wrong. I so wish that was true. She has spent the day throwing up, so they are also going to keep an eye on her for bulimia, as she has lost an incredible amount of weight these past three weeks and I could see her binge eating.

Huge Hug,
Deb

From Exey to Deb:

Dear Deb,

Well, I talked to Jake last night and found out everything. I have to say I'm just relieved she was not in the car. As you know, I've been saying for a long time that she needs help and maybe this was the final wake up call for Jake.

I'm very sad that I'm not there to help you with this. I do feel very grateful that you have found this facility and it sounds good. I do wish I were there for both you and Jake. Monday isn't going to be easy, but these things never are. I know that this is what she has to do to save her life and I know that she is going to be terribly angry, frustrated, hysterical, and very dramatic... but you already know firsthand that is what will save her right now.

I said to Jake, if you need to hide the car from her, you can always keep it at my house. My heart is aching, and of course: All the old feelings of guilt and so on have been racing in my head, so I will be on the phone to my ALANON sponsor in Los Angeles as soon as the time is right.

I can't thank you enough for being there for Natasha and me. You are a great lady and I am forever grateful to you. Please keep in constant touch with me.

I love you.

On Monday morning, we arrived at the facility and something within Natasha just clicked. She knew we were leaving her there and began to sob hysterically in a way that would have softened even the hardest heart.

Jake felt beyond awful while my heart was breaking, but I was glad that we had this chance to save her. I felt that everything I had been through with Haley had prepared me to do the right thing for my other baby and hold a steady course.

Once inside, we were greeted and given the rules. Basically, Natasha was not allowed to talk to us for a week, but after that the phone calls could start and we would be allowed to visit. Amid tears, we left and a week passed. We were informed that Natasha was doing well. The counselors even mentioned that she was a pleasure.

Of course.

She was our sparkle.

The model patient, she was extolling all the lessons she was being taught and was displaying virtues that would make any seasoned member of AA proud. I prayed that this time at rehab would keep her safe for life and she wouldn't fall prey to drug abuse like her big sister.

I just couldn't bear it.

Please God. Not both of my girls.

Later, Natasha told me she felt we had "dropped her off in the ghetto."

Over the course of those 30 days, Natasha really did seem to blossom. She even wrote us lovely letters saying how very sorry she was to have acted so badly over the past couple of years.

Jake and I were relieved and felt the ship of her life was finally on the right course. We helped to save her, which is a parent's job. When she returned home, Natasha told us she would complete all the courses she needed to take to get her high school diploma. Her goal was to eventually move to San Diego to go to City College there with one of her best friends.

We were thrilled because our little girl was thinking clearly about her future.

CHAPTER
FOURTEEN

WHO WAGS THE TAIL?

During this tumultuous time, Haley was trying to get her life in order. She moved back to the area of the intervention to share a house with a couple that looked like they were straight out of Hell's Angels. She signed a six-month lease with them, insisting that they were super nice, and she now considered them family.

She would pay for her rent by working at a local Petco. I felt overjoyed to receive a daily phone call from her telling me how much fun she was having grooming the dogs. I was so grateful that the pieces were falling into place and her cure was there.

She also told me about a pet grooming school she wanted to attend. It cost $3,500 but she would be able to earn decent money once she graduated. This must count as a fishing rod, so I whipped out my trusty credit card and started putting the monthly payments on it. I was so happy for Haley who was really flapping her wings.

A month passed and Jake and I were consumed with visiting Natasha at her rehab. Yes, he did go for those meetings. Meanwhile, life returned to a busy hum, interrupted one day by a call from the lady who owned the pet grooming school. I called her back and we played phone tag for a few days. I called Haley why this woman was phoning me.

"Oh Mom, they let me leave early," Haley said. "I already know how to do the grooming part they were teaching today."

"Oh," I replied, but a sickly feeling settled into my stomach.

Finally, I connected with the owner who informed me that Haley's outlandish behavior in class was unacceptable. "She has an inability to sit still," the owner began. The laundry list of her behaviors went on and on. My stomach lurched because she was describing all the symptoms and behaviors of a demon we knew so well: Crystal Meth.

The bitch was back.

How could I fix her now? I had absolutely no idea. I was once again gobsmacked.

I felt so badly for Jake because all I could do was spend days lying outside, my face buried in the grass. I would sob and sob, my only outlet for unspeakable grief.

My neighbors would later tell me that they could hear me sobbing outside at night. There was no other choice because I was filled with so much anguish. I didn't know how to fight the demon and there was no rulebook called Mom v. Meth.

Untangled and undone, I couldn't push past the sorrow and guilt. John Stenzel and I were in constant contact now. He agreed to meet me for coffee, and I arrived half an hour early to write out my latest ideas. I managed to cover two pages on a legal pad. Yes, I had a new plan. I would ultimately save her with the help of a serious outpatient program Haley told me she would attend.

I had left the cash for her weekly allowance there, as I knew this would definitely make her show up for the first class.

I was making moves against a master chess player.

John read through my list of ideas that day, smiled and said, "Deb, how would you like to organize my life?" However, he didn't seem pleased with my plan for Haley and I was baffled.

"Deb, do nothing," he said.

He may as well have been speaking Chinese to me because what he was saying was so foreign a concept that I didn't even comprehend it. Was this some kind of Zen thing I needed to study? How did one do nothing?

Jake and I were leaving for a vacation the next day and John told me to leave my Blackberry behind. "Just get some rest and relaxation," he said.

I listened to him. It was liberating to be in a different time zone experiencing a quiet type of peace where no horrible phone calls could change the mood in an instant. Two weeks later, we returned home from Costa Rica and the first thing I did was call to see how my daughter was doing in her new outpatient program.

The counselor told me in a matter-of-fact tone that Haley had been in only once and that was to collect the envelope containing the money. Afterwards, she called in each time to cancel. "I'm too busy with work," she had insisted.

I knew that was a lie because her work, and the grooming school, had told me that she was no longer welcome. In fact, they hadn't heard from her in weeks. It was just another stomach punch sucking the wind out of my gut.

Haley had relapsed. She was using meth again.

I could no longer tap dance around the reality.

It was just too much reality.

Nothing prepared me for the waves of shock that went through my body. Howling at the moon didn't work and neither did ripping at my clothes. I thought about taking sleeping pills because they might offer some sweet relief of sleep, but I didn't. My mind raced to comprehend what was happening because it wasn't logical. I had checked the "cured" box in my mind when it came to her illness.

We were back to zero.

Again, I called John. We went around and around, but he insisted that I should "do nothing."

One morning, I was out riding horses to find some solace with Marie by my side. "I read somewhere about nailing Jello to trees," I said. "That's exactly how I feel with my daughters."

Marie chuckled. "Deb, you have nailed every flavor of Jello to every tree in the woods," she said.

John decided that we would go demon destroying again. He suggested an intensive week course at Cottonwood in Arizona, the only place that also had a recovery program for family members. We were just back from vacation and I was hesitant to go away so quickly, but I needed a change. I wanted a different place. And I wanted to understand and learn, plus I needed a respite from my unending torture.

Most of all, I wanted to wage war against the demon that possessed my eldest daughter.

I would become Deb the demon destroyer. I would wear my

silver bracelets like a Wonder Woman and be strong.

Letter to Haley from her Me:

Dear Haley,

I am so sorry your illness has come back. Here are numbers that can help you.

Please find a rent check for July enclosed and a check for Sebastian's board. It's the last one I am paying.

Beg the current ranch to return some of the security deposit. Tell them you can't move without it and beg the grooming school to let you retake the course when you are better.

I will no longer be funding your drug habit. Do not attempt to call me. I have changed my phone numbers. Do not visit. I will call the police. You can call John if you decide you want to choose recovery.

If you see my daughter, tell her I have missed her for many years. I enjoyed meeting her recently. My new philosophy is: Let go, let God.

Love Mom

I also went looking for strength through emails.

From Deb to John:

Hi John :)

I am feeling much stronger today. Sorry, if my email was a bit depressing. I have been re-reading Love First and it has really helped a lot. I understand that I have to take my power back by letting go. I Fedex'd her July rent check and allowance for the week. She will receive it tomorrow.

She offered to be tested (to her sister over the phone) and then said something about running out of her ADD medicine. I wondered if you could recommend a place for her to go to get tested? She is currently living in Chatsworth. I am going to phone her tomorrow and tell her I love her and I'm sorry the illness came back. I'll remind her if she is willing to go into rehab for 90 days, as she agreed before she left RC, and then stay in sober living for nine months, she has my support.

John, she was doing so well, but refused to attend AA meetings or accept any support from a sponsor. She was so excited to attend grooming school. The lady from the school said that Haley could re-enroll once she is sober... somewhere down the road. It sounds like she was totally strung out on the days she was there.

I am so glad you told me to expect this. I understand the need to fully keep her in a program for a year and for Haley to earn the right to share a house and to make her own money. My supporting her really backfired this time. I understand that I have been enabling because it's painful to choose the correct path, but I am ready to be a warrior (with love) to save my daughter.

From John; to Deb:

Hi Deb,

I am out of town on business until Wednesday. If she goes along with you, where are you considering putting her into treatment for 90-days and then sober living for 9-months? I would like to talk to you about that before you make any commitments, please. Also, let's have coffee next week to get our heads together and maybe work through some of the issues. Are you working with Pat or anyone to assist you? If so, I will support you by merely talking. If not, let's work up a plan together.

Warm regards,

John

From Marie to Deb:

Concentrate on this sentence: "To get something you never had, you have to do something you never did."

"When God takes something from your grasp, he's not punishing you, but merely opening your hands to receive something better."

Here's how I read it. You have to let go of "Haley the addict" and realize she has already been taken from your grasp. If you can completely, completely let go then you will be open to receive the "real Haley," your beautiful daughter, when SHE makes her way out of this. Her only way out is on her own. Your rescue efforts cannot help, but rather they can only prolong the amount of time she spends in hell. Her only way out is when SHE truly resolves to make her way out of there.

The doing something you never did part could be enrolling yourself into a program right away and working on changing the co-dependent behaviors and thoughts so that you can be there for her on the other side. She will need you to be as different as she is when she forges her way through this nightmare and comes out on the other side.

Keep a mental picture of a healthy you waiting with open arms for the recovering beautiful girl when she comes out the other side.

Love Marie

From Deb to Marie:

Darling, thanks for putting up with my newly formed habit of "neediness." I ended up driving around yesterday.... just bawling my eyes out. It comes in huge waves. Truly, I never want you to imagine for a second how you would feel if it were your daughter. It's just so much bigger than any words I can find.

Hahaha, I now have to give up mascara and keep the dark shades on. If she were homeless, I could not imagine what would become of her. I guess I am about to find out. Jake was so shocked at my appearance and general state, he has given me his blessing to go for the week to the parent rehab course in Arizona and get whatever help I can. He said I am the strongest person he knows. I am also going to start writing my feelings down again.

I thought of coming over to your office, but that would be most unprofessional, and you give me so much of your love and time already. Maybe we can make time for it when you are feeling teary and we can have a GREAT BIG cry together and shed our tears for the whole of humanity.

Love you loads.
Debxxx

It was a given that I would speak to my neighbor who had been in recovery with AA for many years. And she surprised me, insisting that she was concerned for our safety. "Your daughter is back using," she said. "There is no end to what an addict will do in order to get their fix." She even suggested a restraining order. How could I ever do such a thing?

In the private moments, I branded myself the world's worst

mother. I had two daughters who were swallowing pills. How could I have done this to these girls? Jake wouldn't listen to that theory and told me to "buck up because you're a great Mom." I really appreciated his kind words.

Physically, our family woes were taking a toll, so I went to see my own doctor who diagnosed me with severe stress disorder. The symptoms included this tingling up and down my arms and occasional hyperventilating. I was a mess.

Part of my own therapy was writing this in my diary:

Thank you, my daughters. It will take every piece of knowledge I can lay my hands on to heal myself. Right at this moment, my pain seeps from every pore.

I suck as a Mother.

I have no influence or discipline with either of you anymore. I participated in all of your activities, loved you both more than life, fed you, and nursed you.

Not enough.

Where is the handbook that should have come with you both?

Where is my wisdom?

CHAPTER
FIFTEEN

ARIZONA

It was John, earth angel to the max, who spoke with the counselors at Cottonwood. Immediately, they had a room for me. There would be no more excuses. The world would keep turning with me gone for another week.

I got on the plane.

My arrival in Arizona was marked by a few cactus sightings outside the bus that took us to the rehab hospital. Glancing around, I gazed at about 30 people from every background and walk of life. What linked us was the commonality of our pain, which leveled any difference in age, gender or worldly success.

I became a person of curiosity because I wasn't visiting a patient at the hospital. I was the one seeking recovery for my life, yet it was still hard for the other participants to understand why I would put myself through this boot camp.

There would be the inevitable questions as to why I was there, and I didn't want to rain on anyone's hope. I had no idea if their sons or daughters would relapse, but I prayed that they would all make it – as much for the parents as their children/relatives.

During our sessions, each person hung on every word that came from that counselor's mouth. We believed they had the secret of absolution for our loved ones, or maybe for us. We were a group of wounded and puzzled souls looking for any answers.

I ate dinner on my own during this time in order to work on my homework and grapple with the "what I don't know" part of the therapy. Expanding my brain was key because both of my daughters needed me to have this new knowledge.

There were no unkind judgments from the fellow humans in this place of possible answers. No finger pointing. No blame. We had all walked at least a mile in each other's shoes; we knew first-hand how uncomfortable and distressing the fit was when those shoes became vice grips.

I wondered if maybe those wise counselors had a self-help book for deranged mothers. One of the moms I met there described us as the two shards of glass. It was absolutely accurate in that we were sharp and so broken.

I should mention that when I unpacked, I found a note from my daughter Natasha that she asked me to read in Arizona. The envelope read:

> *By the way, good luck DebMama,*
> *Feel better.....everything is going to be okay.*
> *I promise.*
> *I love you so very much,*
> *Love Natasha.*
> *PS: Bring this envelope with you. I love you and appreciate you so much,*
> *DebMama, please get better.*

The letter filled me with joy.

Dear DebMama:

I love you more than anything. You are a great Mom.

Never forget that and don't let anyone tell you differently. You are the reason I have always had a big smile on my face. Your kindness/happiness rubs off on people and so does your sadness. It's so hard to see.

What I thought was the happiest lady on earth is sooooo sad. What's happening? You are an extremely loving woman with only good intentions.

You have a giant heart!!

Remember to be strong, relax and to enjoy your life. You only get one. The world is too beautiful for you to look and feel so shitty.

Everything is going to be okay.

Get better. I love you.

Natasha.

I taped this to my folder to give me strength from my baby girl. She drew me pictures of rainbows, butterflies, flowers, and sunshine and said they all resembled me to her.

What a precious gift Natasha gave me.

In Arizona, our counselor Eddie, an amazing individual, divided us into small groups. We were a mixture of family members and actual addict patients, which made for an interesting mix. Mine included a relapsed young mother who was on her second time here in rehab. The first time, her husband and parents stayed for the family week.

This time around, she was facing it alone; by choice, shadowed by only her own courage.

The third family was comprised of a young woman in her early 20s who had issues with her mother, plus feared abandonment. Her father and sister were right there for support. As time passed, we became increasingly comfortable with each other.

These were such soul bearing and gut-wrenching days that were flooded with tears. At night, we worked on our homework that would be shared the next day. One assignment asked me to fill out certain lists.

List of Concerns for Haley:

These are my thoughts, feelings, and perceptions. The choice to change is yours and mine.

When you relapsed two weeks ago, I felt desolate, fear and hurt.

When you phone me over and over begging for money, I feel fear, anger and sadness.

When you lie -- like the time a few weeks ago when you said they had let you out of school early -- I felt fear, sadness and hurt.

When you break your promises -- like the time two weeks ago when you rescheduled your initial outpatient appointment three times -- I felt fear, anger and sadness.

When you blame me -- like when we spoke last -- I felt guilt, shame and sadness.

List of Appreciations for Haley:

*When you take charge of your responsibilities -- like the time in January when you got the full-time job -- I feel proud, grateful and hopeful.

*When you do things that are thoughtful -- like the time you thanked me for hanging in there -- I felt grateful, hopeful and happy.

*When you use your talents -- like that time I saw you and Sebastian winning a ribbon and participating -- I felt grateful, hopeful and proud.

*When you say funny things -- like you did about the car or lack of it last year -- I felt hopeful, grateful and relieved.

*When you remember special days -- like this past Mother's Day -- I felt hopeful, happy, and grateful.

Goals/Commitments For My Daughters

*What I will do to build a healthier relationship is set and maintain healthy boundaries in our relationships.

*What I will do for my recovery is to begin one-on-one counseling in two weeks to address my own issues, plus parents' Al-Anon, and CODA.

*Something special I will do for myself is (within a week of returning home) I will ride my horse, Sampson, at least four times a week.

Boundaries:

*For my well-being, I can't continue enabling. I will not provide any more money, other than for additional treatment.

*For my well-being, if you continue to use, I will ask you not to contact me for two months or until I feel comfortable and you test clean and free of drugs.

*If you arrive at my home and verbally or physically abuse me or any other family member, I will call the police and get a restraining order.

We had to read our list to the group each day. Eddie warned, "Deb, I know this will be hard for you." When I read mine, I was sobbing my heart out. With confidence, I said at the end, "I will do this. I will no longer be a drug dealer."

I was told to write a letter to my daughters.

Letter to My Daughters:

I would like you to know that I unconditionally love you beyond time. You were a precious angel sent down for me to care for.

I have learned that you can't be micromanaged into sobriety; the dignity of your recovery is yours alone.

I have learned that I did not know where you ended and I began. By being an enabler, I was your drug dealer.

I want and need you to dig deep and find a piece of you that is ready to fight for your recovery and then to keep a soft heart. You need to search for your own serenity.

I am willing to give you my unending love, my support for your recovery and whatever is left on my credit cards to pay for treatment.

I ask you to forgive me for rescuing, fixing, always paying and loving you in an unhealthy way. I was trying to be the wind beneath your wings, but there was never a lift off. Any hurt or pain over the years I have caused you adds to my guilt and fear.

I am willing to forgive myself for trying too hard to make your life perfect, damaging your wings, not being able to keep you safe and happy or protected. I loved you in an unhealthy way and did so by killing you with kindness. At the same time, I was taking all the sorrow, grief, and fear into my body. It's too heavy and I am putting it down now.

As I got ready to leave, I felt so good about the young woman who had relapsed and was back for a second time. She gave me such hope that maybe it would be possible for my daughters to choose sobriety.

There was a graduation day at the end of my stay and all family members, patients and staff assembled for the ceremony. We received a chip to keep and each member of our smaller group was asked to speak about what the week had taught them. I was so grateful for the unspeakable amounts of guidance.

And so, I returned home with new tools to call upon. I reflected on all that I learned, knowing one of the most important lessons was to forgive myself or at least to work on trying to give myself a break.

I had done the best for my girls with the information I had at the time.

I didn't know what I didn't know. I liked that saying because it was okay to not know a whole lot. It's called being human.

I was also taught how to man up.

The wimp was gone. Or, at least, I would not let my daughters see me being a wimp.

CHAPTER SIXTEEN

CHANGES

The trip home from Arizona might have been an omen. It was one of those white-knuckle flights with the plane bouncing up and down, which left me queasy. I also felt dead tired. I knew that in a few days, Natasha was leaving home to go to the City College in San Diego, just hours away.

A huge moving truck showed up at our house on Saturday morning, organized by a thoughtful friend's Mom. At school, Natasha was sharing a house with another one of her best friends who was one of the good influences, so we were happy and hopeful. A change of scenery would be good for her.

It felt good to hit the ground running at home. I was helping Natasha squish things into boxes and the moving men were everywhere. Who knew that she had that much stuff? As for our girl, she had been on best behavior for the past few months since she left rehab. I knew we caught her in time and prevented a future disaster.

Eventually, the truck left, and I opened the door to her room.

Oh, it hit me like a ton of bricks. Just dust balls on the floor. No bed. No baby.

Nothing prepared me for the emotional roller coaster of an empty nest. I tried the stiff upper lip, but I felt devastated.

I was very happy for Natasha and excited that the house she was moving into was right next to the beach. I could picture my baby watching sunsets as I mourned the loss of watching them with her. A child leaving the nest is such a sad rite of passage for the parents and it was proving challenging for me.

It was just Jake and me.

Both numb and edgy.

As time progressed, I got better at the "do nothing" part of addict mothering and stopped the food allowance for Haley. A mad meth addict turning up on my doorstep was frightening and I had reason to believe she had scaled the gates before, haunting our garden late at night.

With my boundaries in place, I changed my phone number, gate code, cell phone number and email address. It was the first of many changes. The phone company must have thought I was a nut, as this happened a few times over the next several months. Even I had no idea what my number was on a day-to-day basis.

Jake was so enraged during this period that he became a one-man swearing squad. All I heard was "fuck this, fuck that." I hate hearing swear words even though I have indulged in the occasional "fuck" when it came to my daughters' antics. Finally, I asked Jake to speak to me in a beautiful way, preferably with a "darling" before or after each sentence. It was time to raise the quality of our exchanges or bring them back to where they started when we were fresh and new as a couple.

I didn't get the answer I expected.

"Well, then we'll just have silence," Jake said.

"Perfection," I replied.

When I wasn't busy changing my phone number, I spent my time digging out my frustrations in my garden. It was a great way to lose myself in the hope of creating something beautiful. I needed an outlet because I missed my daughters like someone who craved breathing. Watering plants while crying probably wasn't the perfect solution, but it filled the hours.

There were moments when I felt as if we had finally figured out a plan. Just when I could find an ounce of hope, a tidal wave of uncontrollable grief would hit me. One day, I was driving and called Marie. Through huge gulps and sobs, I told her I felt like driving into a telegraph pole.

"Go to the nearest bookstore and buy anything to do with meditation and Dr. Wayne Dyer," she advised.

I found myself in the self-help section of Borders (crying), but through blurred vision I grabbed all the CDs Marie instructed me to collect. Why wait? I ripped them open and listened on the way home as Dr. Dyer's soothing voice came over my car stereo.

Oh my God! What a life changer. I had a new car friend and I couldn't get enough of his wisdom.

I called Marie and asked, "What's the DOW? Is it the stock exchange?"

She laughed gently. "No Deb, it's the Tao and it has to do with meditation." The good doc encouraged me on one CD to find a quiet, special spot and just be still. I hadn't been still in decades.

Suddenly, I knew exactly what to do with part of Natasha's empty bedroom. Jolted with renewed energy, I changed the upstairs loft into my own personal meditation area. It didn't cost much beyond a $20 beanbag and a $10 Buddha statue from World Market. Buddha was actually on sale that week.

I hung my chip from my experience at Cottonwood around his neck. I would add a small fountain, wind chimes and pictures of my girls, friends and family to the mix. Then there was that bright pink riding crop, shaped like a star that became my magic wand. I would read a mantra each morning, sending my girls sobriety, peace, serenity and a whole other laundry list that parents wish for our children.

Happy and safe.

That's all we want.

I also practiced a meditation for well-being that I brought home from Cottonwood in Arizona.

Meditation for Well Being

*The beauty of this meditation is that you add whatever or whomever you want inside the parenthesis. Repeat these words:

(1)

May I (my children) be happy.

May I (they) be safe.

May I (they) be healthy.

May I (they) live in ease and well-being.

May I (they) be free from suffering.

May I (they) live in loving kindness.

(2)

May I (they) be happy.

May I (they) be safe from all danger and harm.

May I (they) be healthy in body and mind.

May I (they) live in ease and well-being.

May I (they) be free from suffering.

May I (they) live in loving-kindness.

May they be of service.

May they always have angels walking beside them.

(3)

Substitute "I" with "You" (thinking of someone), and then "We" (thinking of relationships, community), and then "All beings".

Chant the affirmations in one breath (if possible): Inhale and chant (1) as you exhale. Inhale and repeat for several minutes; then chant (2) for several minutes; then (3).

I began to include myself in this meditation, which I followed by reading thoughts on enabling behavior or how to keep my oars in my own boat. Both would become a lifelong practice that I still do to this day.

There was an afternoon when I found myself at a store called Ross where I found a statue of a girl with long, dark hair and angel wings. It looked just like Haley to me. In the checkout line, I pulled out my wallet and put the angel statue down on the counter. I couldn't believe it when her wings dropped off.

I knew this must be a sign.

Marie advised me to put that broken angel statue in my meditation area as a symbol because one day my baby girl would glue her wings back on, too.

My baby girl, Haley, was still MIA. The core of my sorrow revolved around the pain of not knowing where my daughter was living or how she was managing. Night terrors consumed me as I had visions of her lost and alone on the streets.

If only I could reach out to her, but that wasn't possible.

All I had was that little broken statue.

CHAPTER SEVENTEEN

VISITORS

My cousin visited me from the UK with his young family and we actually had a lovely family afternoon at home. We were outside looking at the gardens when suddenly the dogs started barking like crazy and a feeling of dread crept up over me. Walking past our tall hedges, I blinked a few times in total disbelief.

My daughter stood in front of me.

Rail thin with a marked face and greasy hair, Haley was smiling gently. Her shaking hands held a bunch of red roses and a card. "I got these for you, Mom," she said with tears welling in her eyes.

Oh my God! How do I detach, but not abandon?

"You can't be here, Haley," I told her and with each word, my heart broke a little deeper.

At least she was alive.

My mind raced because I didn't want my cousin's children to see her this way because much too much explaining would be required. I didn't want them to be scared by her appearance or demeanor.

There was no space for this reunion.

In the end, Haley left, and I threw the flowers and the card in our big dumpster. I felt as if my heart was covered in cement.

Marie offered to come over and dig the card out. She wanted to read it to me. "No point," I told her. "It's just the demon writing to me. I don't want to hear the demon's words."

Oh, how my heart ached.

Everything inside of me wanted to grab Haley, lock her in a cupboard, and keep her safe where I could take care of her. I kept repeating over and over again, "The dignity of her recovery is hers alone. I may not interfere."

It was counter intuitive parenting.

I had to obtain an official restraining order to bar my daughter from legally visiting me. Obtaining it is one of those horrible life experiences on all levels. I didn't know which paperwork to fill out and the clerks ignored my "I'm nice" smile and made the process as difficult as possible. I wandered from long line to long line wishing that I had someone, anyone, to hold my hand.

"I am a warrior and I am saving my child," I reminded myself. "I am in the battle!"

That helped a bit.

There were other soul-destroying moments of banning my child including a procedure where I had to go upstairs in the courtroom and appear in front of a judge who would then grant the temporary restraining order. Court closed at four p.m. and I had to run there on a busy day. Deep inside, I was filled with doubt and still wondered if I was doing the right thing. I didn't realize that I would be asked questions about my daughter and the order I was seeking from a very stern-faced judge. Tears began to roll down my face; I had zero control over my emotions.

Ultimately, the order was granted, and the court clerk walked toward me.

"You're doing the right thing," she said.

"But it hurts so much," I cried.

"I wish my mother would have done this for my brother a long time ago," she added. My gratitude for these words and her kindness remains boundless.

A soft rain was falling as I left that courtroom, the perfect touch given my current mood. That day in court when I officially got a restraining order with my daughter's name on it would go down as a new all-time low moment in my life.

It was a long, slow drive home and I kept repeating to myself, "I am Deb, the demon destroyer. I am strong. I am a good Mom. Oh, please, please, let there be a piece of my daughter left alive inside of her body. Let us find a piece that is willing to fight for her life, so that she comes back to me and herself."

As instructed, I taped the sheriff's number to all our phones.

Later, Haley would tell me that she was at a loss for words and in complete shock when the sheriff served her that restraining order.

The night terrors made sleep impossible although my addled brain continued to conjure up every awful scenario including my daughter being held against her will or being abused in return for drugs.

Someone make it stop.

Almost total sleep deprivation made me unable to complete even the most mundane, normal tasks. There were even fleeting moments when my slurry of a brain thought it might be better if she were dead. I could actually bury her and know she was safe. In another more lucid moment, I was shocked I had these thoughts. How could I? How dare I? Please, forgive me.

When I went back to court again, I made the restraining order permanent. It was another horrible experience I would never wish on any parent. This is not what you dream about when you hold that newborn baby and dip your toe in all those dreams.

That day, I met Marie at the Cheesecake Factory known for its enormous desserts. I ordered just one slice of cherry cheesecake, knowing it was big enough to feed several people. I called it my entrée and ignored the stares of the other customers. It didn't take long until the sugar kicked in and I felt my blood rush. How lucky am I to have such an amazing friend for these kinds of moments?

Post-order, life became about digging in the garden, meditating and communing with my animals. I even sang, although not well, but loudly. *Amazing Grace* was my tune of choice and it stuck in my head like it was on a loop. I heard it on one of Dr. Dyer's CDs along with the old classic, Row Your Boat. Your "own" boat became the key part. This song was very hard for me because I always wanted to lend my oar or maybe steer for you while not noticing that my personal boat is headed right over the churning rapids.

One of my friends emailed me the following "teaching" and I printed it out and taped it to the inside of the cupboard door.

Lessons on Life

There was a man who had four sons. He wanted his sons to learn not to judge things too quickly. So, he sent them each on a quest, in turn, to go and look at a pear tree that was a great distance away.

The first son went in the winter, the second in the spring, the third in the summer and the youngest son in the fall.

When they had all gone and come back, he called them together to describe what they had seen.

The first son said that the tree was ugly, bent, and twisted. The second son said no, it was covered with green buds and full of promise.

The third son disagreed; he said it was laden with blossoms that smelled so sweet and looked so beautiful. It was the most graceful thing he had ever seen.

The last son disagreed with all of them; he said it was ripe and drooping with fruit, full of life, and fulfillment.

The man then explained to his sons that they were all right, because they had each seen but only one season in the tree's life.

He told them that you cannot judge a tree, or a person, by only one season, and that the essence of who they are and the pleasure, joy, and love that comes from that life can only be measured at the end, when all the seasons are up.

If you give up when it's winter, you will miss the promise of your spring, the beauty of your summer, and fulfillment of your fall.

Moral: Don't let the pain of one season destroy the joy of all the rest. Don't judge life by one difficult season. Persevere through the difficult patches and better times are sure to come.

I prayed I would see a good season of my daughter's life soon.

As time passed, I continued to sing and although our home was very private and surrounded by trees, I knew my neighbors could clearly hear me. They were saints for never complaining about my warbling singing voice. In hindsight, it was probably preferable to my sobbing.

Seasons passed and people stopped asking about Haley. I told them I just couldn't talk about it anymore. The truth was I didn't have anything left to say. Why tell the same sad story over and over again when there wasn't even a glimmer of a happy ending?

I could only wait.

Along the way, I brushed up against my 50th birthday. It was significant, so I decided to decorate Natasha's empty room, the one apart from the already decorated meditation area in the loft. What it needed was obvious! I bought a disco ball! And flashing lights! Joy! I knew this would totally change the vibe in the room and help me not feel Natasha's departure so acutely each time I went in there.

Then the phone rang, but this time it was good news. Natasha was calling to say she would be home for my birthday. I broke the news about her room, and she laughed loudly. In a blink, she was home and visiting/inspecting the meditation area.

"It's a little weird, but I like it," she said.

Maybe it was weird, but it saved my life and does to this day.

"It looks like your brain exploded up there," Jake told me.

Maybe it did.

I had a kickass 50th disco birthday. Everyone avoided mentioning Haley's name although I missed her. Desperately.

A little of my sun returned and the cup became half full again.

Natasha was the ultimate present.

CHAPTER EIGHTEEN

SECOND CHANCES

Months passed and John was my rock. He visited Haley when we discovered where she was living and even took her for groceries. He also encouraged her to re-enter rehab for 90 days. He asked for absolutely nothing in return. He valued her as a human, and there were no words that could express my gratitude.

Who else would care about someone else's child in this way? I knew that God had sent John to us. He walked the talk with integrity, humanity and compassion.

It seemed like an eternity as months passed and there was no news of Haley. She refused to return John's phone calls although he never stopped reaching out to her. Some of the return phone calls from her sounded like they came from the creature in *The Exorcist*.

Letter from John to Haley:

Dear Haley,

I hope this note finds you well and with some food in your stomach. I know these times can be pretty scary. I am here for you. But you have to make these difficult decisions yourself. I will be here to support you and get you up to Santa Barbara if and when you are ready to do so on Tuesday. I encourage you to do it.

A couple of things:

Here is the key for the storage unit that you and I picked out on Friday along with a card that has the code to get into the public storage gate.

When you put your things in storage, please also include all the equipment for your horse too, the saddle and anything else. It would be best stored for now.

If you do decide to put all your things in storage and are willing and ready to go into rehab in Santa Barbara for 90 days, you can call me so I can make arrangements to have your horse taken to your Mom's house, which she has agreed to do.

Also, as far as your truck, I will make arrangements to have it stored while you are in Santa Barbara. We will need to meet somewhere on Tuesday, very early, and I will take the keys and transfer it later after you are safe in Santa Barbara.

I wish you well. Hope to hear from you this weekend.
John

Again, I felt a twinge of renewed hope surging through my system. Would she choose her salvation? I prayed that my girl would be saved and those 90 days would mend everything. I waited for an unbearably long weekend to unfold, so John could drive her to the rehab on Monday morning.

I received this email on Sunday evening.
From John to Deb:

Hi Deb,

A quick note... I conversed with Haley yesterday several times, but the last voicemail I received from her last night basically said she had decided to move to Santa Ynez with a trainer friend of hers today. She was taking her horse and dogs. She said that they had secured a place to go live. She said she was attending an NA meeting last night, and the first thing they would be doing in Santa Ynez is to attend a NA meeting there.

I will try and call you later on today. I have a family obligation this morning that will keep me tied up until noon or so, but will get in touch with you then so we can talk.

Keep a good thought; we are not finished with all of this. Haley sounds fine for now. Hang in there. It is in God's hands too.

Warm regards,
John

So, she had once again slipped from my grasp, bolting away at the last moment. My daughter was becoming a ghost.

Some weeks later I received a forwarded email from a friend of a friend:

Hi R (my neighbor),

I am so sorry to put you in the middle of whatever is going on with Haley. A lady called for Deb's number and I don't have her new contact information. I thought you could give it to her.

If I could ask you one more thing, could you forward this

on to Deb?

She would like Haley's horse removed from the property. She will reimburse any money owed and will even deliver the horse to the new location.

I'm sorry that I have to ask you this.

People still managed to get these messages to me. I heard from a friend of a friend of a friend that my daughter was now homeless in a town a few hours away. She was homeless with her horse. The humane thing to do was to hook up my trailer and go rescue him. What about my daughter?

My friends wanted to go. Should we? Should I react? Too much was depending on this moment. My boundaries actually rescued me. I got word back to Haley that I wouldn't be available for anything until she willingly chose 90 days in rehab. With those words, I changed my phone number again.

I told Jake. "I wish all my news came by carrier pigeon."

From John to Deb:

Hi Deb,

Thought I would check in with you and say hello. I have not had any phone calls from Haley this week and was wondering if you have?

Based on her last several voicemails, I don't suspect I will be getting any from her either. She pretty much said she had lost all trust in me because of what she believes went down with Anne and that it was all my fault that Anne and her husband asked Haley to leave the horse barn. I spoke to Anne following, to get some clarification, and she said absolutely not. It was just the drugs and the addiction talking. She said Haley needed someone to blame for her not being able to stay there and it wasn't going to be Anne. I feel bad about that because I worked pretty hard to build what level of trust I thought there was between Haley and me, but can't control how she feels, nor can I worry about it either.

So, hope you are doing well and will stay in contact, too. I want to get you the extra key and code card for the public storage. I still pray that Haley will eventually understand the need for treatment.

Warm regards,

John

To John from Deb:

Hey John,

I'm sorry Haley left you nasty phone calls, but it's the demon talking and not her. As a fighter of demons, I spent all day Monday at Van Nuys court and had the restraining order made permanent for three years.

Today I picked up a friend's little one, Kelsey, from school and was on my way home with her and saw a car coming through the air, upside down in slow motion and land- smoke billowing out of it. I parked, told Kelsey to stay in the car and started running towards the car. I called 911 and was on the phone with them forever. To my great joy, I saw one person getting out of the car and she pulled the other person out of the car. I got them to sit in the shade and I guess it took 15 minutes for paramedics to arrive. It felt like forever. People actually drove past and around the smoking car. Can you believe they didn't stop to help?

Kelsey and I went home and groomed my miniature horses and I told my friend she probably would never let me take Kelsey again. I am so grateful they were alive, John. The car was scrunched up worse than the one at Lost Hills Sherriff station. They both looked about 16 or 17. I am very distressed this evening and tired, but I know what to do. We have to keep our strength up for fighting demons, I'm so glad I am on your team :)

Huge hug, much love,

Deb

From Deb to John:

Just an adage, this metamorphosis is only possible because at long last, I have God beside me.

From John to Deb:

That's better.

From Marie to Deb:

I've been home thinking of you… I felt so horrible leaving you, and felt so torn with my kids at home feeling so neglected… I won't be home again until late Friday night and I so wish I could have been two places at once. I wanted to just put you in my pocket and take you with me.

I hope by now you are sleeping, and it will all feel better in the morning. When you were telling me about how John and Haley haven't been in touch, it made me feel like just driving straight up to Solvang and roaming around until I found her… and bringing her home for safe keeping.

I don't know how you are finding the strength to go through this, I really don't…. but deep down I guess I do know. God made a mother's love stronger than anything on the planet, and when put to the test, that love can give us the strength to

do all manner of things that we never imagined we might --
physically, emotionally, or financially. Somehow you just reach
way down and find it, and that's exactly what you're doing.

I was thinking too... Just as you were there like an angel
for those two involved in the car accident, for your friend's
daughter, for your neighbor and her horse, and for me (like
you are every day), there are angels and mothers out there
everywhere. Just keep picturing a healthy, smiling Haley who
has freed herself from the demon, and trust that God has his
plan and his angels are strategically placed -- the right one at
the right time will deliver her safely to rehab when she's ready.

Your thoughts and your mental pictures are important.
Taking good care of yourself includes choosing positive
thoughts. Your positive thoughts and your "intention" to see
her healthy and smiling will make it happen. I know I keep
saying this, but I really do believe it.
Call me tomorrow-
With love,
Marie

There were many months of silence and then the whole world
seemingly changed. I wrote John the following note:

Hey John :),

I hope your weekend was excellent!

I am CC-ing Natasha on this email as I have asked her to
give you a call with an update...

Natasha visited with Haley yesterday and it seems
everything Haley told you is true. She is renting a room in
a house. She is working at least two jobs. She has Sebastian
there and told Natasha she pays $600 for rent and $300 for
Sebastian's board (wow! huge progress!) Natasha can explain

in detail where she thinks Haley is at, but she said that her sister seems to have really matured a lot! The news of Haley from Natasha gave me a good few hours of sobbing my heart out. I feel like I am melting.

Haley's main concern was that she doesn't want to be on her own for the holidays... I am confused as to what the right thing to do is. Maybe, if Haley will get tested for the next four weeks, and if they're clean, she can come over for Thanksgiving and then weekly until Christmas. Then, possibly, I can see her weekly for lunch as long as she keeps her part of our new relationship in continuing to be tested. If she misses even one week then I won't see her again until four clean consecutive tests are in... Does this sound logical?
Huge hug,
Deb

I wasn't prepared for a brand-new set of boundaries that left me feeling dazed, confused and very blonde. Brilliantly, John suggested an outpatient program close to where Haley was now living. They would drug test her regularly and randomly. As the new boundaries began to take shape, if she wanted a relationship with me, she would need to agree to be tested randomly every week, indefinitely, and see the outpatient counselor. Looking back, the one thing that does not lie is a drug test.

With John's encouragement and the new boundaries set in place, my daughter re-entered our lives.

From Deb to John:

Hey there John :),
I hope you are home safe and sound and have maybe caught your breath! Haley is going to sign a release at the

outpatient program tonight, so that the counselor can discuss her case/progress with you.

I chatted with the counselor for a bit today. She said Haley is having problems with a Higher Power and body issues/ weight. I told the counselor that I would not participate in the family program until next Friday. I also asked Haley if you could take her to your doctor for the brain evaluation and she said yes. Woo Hoo!

Haley is coming over tomorrow and spending the night. Let's hope Jake doesn't implode.
Big hug,
Gratefully yours,
Deb

I wrote the following note to Marie.

From Deb to Marie:

I want you to come over and see my little holiday tree, maybe tomorrow after work? It looks rather surprisingly festive, even though Jake is like the Grinch. I had Natasha and Haley over for dinner and Jake yelled at Haley for sitting in his chair before dinner. She reacted so calmly and sweetly, quickly moved to the point that he was actually embarrassed and then told her she did not have to move immediately.

I told her I wanted to kidnap her and just lock her in a cupboard, so I would know she was safe, sort of like a box stall, but no turnouts. She had a good laugh over that. I am so grateful."

From Deb to Marie:

Oh my God, you would have peed your pants laughing. By the time I threw the chicken in the oven, it was PITCH black. I am scared of rats and still had to feed and clean. I am out there with my coalminers light on swearing that I must feed the horses carrots and that I would not be scared if I knew who walked beside me! I swear, putting my hand inside the rat's Four Seasons Hotel (also known as the feed shed) to switch the light on was beyond scary... to get those blasted carrots!

The horses thought I was beyond scary as the one-eyed monster walking around... sounding like me, but my one-eyed light flickered on and off. I made it! I was so happy, I even looked up and the stars were AMAZING! My stepson was here. Of course I love to see him, but he's allowed to do his laundry here and Haley isn't. I know it sounds petty, but it just fries my brain. Haley came over to eat and Jake treated her like a weird relative you are "super forced" to be nice to for a limited period of time.

Marie, she played the vet game on my computer she bought from Bright Star store,and she kept getting all the diagnoses correct! I was dazzled. She is still like an embryo though. I just sense her brightness, but she is so vulnerable, lonely and prickly. She was so happy to have a home cooked meal. I feel like kidnapping her and taking a position in Montana for both of us.

From Marie to Deb:

ROFL!!!

You are hysterical... I only wish we had a movie of that. It could be a big hit on YouTube! We could put together film clips *like when I was parking your trailer down below and left you hanging from a tree, and when we couldn't get Sam's head in the trailer to close the window, and when Mr. P and I pinned you beneath the branch... haha, only you, Pippi!*

I just ran into Haley in the driveway when I ran out to pick up Taylor! :) I'm glad she had a nice dinner. Regular family dinners are good, and a normal thing to do, so Jake should really get used to it. It really doesn't matter if Jake realizes it or not, but she really is coming along nicely... baby steps. She is really trying hard and the progress is absolutely huge! That's the important part. That's what is real. She is holding down a real job. She has a start of horse clients. And she is becoming accountable! She is rowing, she really is...

Xoxo,
Marie

One day, I took Haley up to my meditation area and she told me that she found it comforting. She even confessed that she felt I didn't care anymore about her. When I went to Al-Anon, she made the group sound as if I joined some weird cult that influenced me to walk away from her. I just had to show her that she wasn't abandoned.

It was interesting to hear her viewpoint of the same situation. Her tangible feelings of abandonment were different from mine of tough love to help her survive.

Back at home, there was another view to consider. The inequity of how the now sober Haley was being treated by Jake made me queasy.

He really knew how to put the "step" in stepchild.

CHAPTER NINETEEN

BUTTERFLIES

Time passed and I continued to watch Haley's progress. I was pleasantly surprised when she invited me to visit her home. It was a rundown trailer on a horse farm. I could hardly turn around in there. I did notice a note pinned above her bed (which was all of ten inches from the ceiling). It went along the lines of the following:

> I am a child of God,
> I am strong and sober.
> I am worthwhile.
> I am good.
> I am kind.
> I deserve kindness.

I don't know how I made it out of her trailer without bursting into tears in front of her. Oh, my baby. So, so fragile. She was trying so hard to flap her damaged wings. My daughter's life reminded me of a story I once heard about a man who saw a beautiful butterfly pushing hard against its chrysalis to get out. The man wanted to help the butterfly and took it upon himself to cut open the chrysalis. But wait, the butterfly now had damaged wings and it couldn't fly.

In life, we need the pain of breaking out of our own chrysalis in order to have strong enough wings to fly. In other words, parents with scissors should be avoided at all costs.

My new motto was one day at a time. Don't berate her. This was just a hiccup or her ongoing fight against her evil twin. At the same time, I would not lose myself anymore in that bottomless place of gut wrenching, searing pain. Let it go, let God.

Haley's immediate health concerned me. When it rained, her roof leaked through the holes in that old trailer and I couldn't bear to think of her lying on a wet mattress. What if she got bronchitis again? This reminded me of an incident when both of my daughters were in urgent care at the same time. Natasha had damaged her knee when a friend pulled away before she was out of the car. Her poor leg was filled with three-day-old gravel. Despite the pain, she had chosen not to tell us until three days later. The doctors had to reopen the wound to clean it out, which was horribly awful. Meanwhile, Haley was on a drip due to severe bronchitis.

Literally, I was running from one room in urgent care to the other because both girls were yelling for their Mom.

As for present day Haley, her leaky roof problem solved itself when she was asked to move in with her friend Mark. I really liked him and loved the fact that sober people were showing up in her life without me lifting a finger.

Why was I still feeling vaguely uneasy around her?

"Respond to her phone calls. Do not react," I told myself. It wasn't long before I unconsciously began waiting until the end of the day to listen to any of her messages. Miraculously, more and more of her problems began to solve themselves.

Her new roommate Mark said that living with Haley was like sharing a home with Lucy or Ellie May. He loved that she was the only girl he knew who could smell worse than him at the end of the day. He worked as a mechanic! He also marveled that Haley was still able to dress it up and look like a drop-dead knockout when needed. He told me about the night when he knocked on Haley's bedroom door. He found her sitting in bed and the covers were moving.

"Haley, I thought we agreed. No more pets," he said.

Apparently, she had rescued a homeless dog and was trying to hide it under a comforter.

It turns out Mark should have been nominated for sainthood. He didn't only live with Haley, but also bunked with a variety of God's four-legged creatures including her rescued baby goat (rejected at birth by his Mom). She was spending money she didn't have on special formula milk from Whole Foods and had to take the goat with her everywhere.

I didn't know if I was mad or proud.

There was the day when Haley left me with the baby goat that was frolicking in some green grass. My daughter went to visit the restroom and that baby goat's eyes followed her the entire way. His eyes didn't move until she reappeared while the goat made this "a---aaaaa m-aaaaa" call. I swear he was calling her Ma.

The same day I showed Haley a wonderful sober living community in San Patrignano, Italy. Marie had told me about, and it was actually free. I could hardly comprehend that wonderful fact. Marie and I thought we might like to go there for a vacation. I even asked Haley if she wanted to travel a bit.

"Look, darling," I said, pointing to the website. "They have an equestrian team and a lot of different opportunities." On their webpage was the founder's speech and it remains one of the most moving views of sobriety I have ever heard. I wanted to book Haley a plane ticket.

"Hot Italian men, darling," I said.

She was not impressed. "Mom, look, they grow grapes. That makes wine. That's not very sober."

And so, I dropped the latest idea.

During this time, I thought I was plagued with some sort of strange disease. My days were filled with visiting different doctors and taking tests. Did I have Lyme's Disease? Maybe Epstein Barr? I lost my voice, so I went to an ear and nose specialist who said nothing was really wrong. The best diagnosis was post- traumatic stress.

A creative spark did ignite within and I began writing.

I wondered if Haley had found any outside interests, but she said "no" when I asked if she was dating or going out at all. Her tone didn't invite further questioning from me. Immediately, I felt sad and imagined her life without a partner. She wisely reminded me to keep my oars in my own boat. Sweetly, she reminded me that she didn't need any help at the moment. "I'm busy working on myself, Mom," she said. "What part of that don't you understand?"

I laughed. I got it.

Another time, I asked if she wanted me to spell check her Facebook page, which was filled with typos. "No thank you, Mom," she replied. "This is who I am."

Now, I really got it.

You go, girl!

A sense of calm settled into my bones and I allowed my imagination to blossom. I was starting to really enjoy my relationship with my sisters in arms. It had only taken a village.

Haley called me one afternoon to tell me that she felt that "being of service" was important and she chose to work with young people who had learning disabilities and addiction challenges. She would also help with rescue horses.

Wow!

As a Mom, I couldn't keep my oars in my boat any longer. The irresistible urge to stand up in my boat, rock around wildly, oars atop my head trying to reach Haley's boat overcame me. I enrolled her in an online equestrian dating site, wrote about her interests and listed what she looked for in a partner. I felt positively exuberant. Isn't this how people met each other these days?

I didn't have to wait very long.

Of course, Haley embodied a very mad hornet as she spluttered into the phone line.

"Mom what the f%$#?"

"What darling?" I replied, wondering if I could feign innocence.

Haley exploded. "I'm getting random texts from men I don't know! Really Mom? Really!"

A feeling of shame entered my system. Maybe my brilliant idea was lacking in brilliance. I deactivated the account immediately.

Recovery for parents is also an ongoing process.

I pulled my oars back into my own boat and placed them in the resting position.

I had to learn to allow Haley to be that free butterfly. There would always be things I didn't approve of including bouncing into our house with her pants regularly ripped. I tried to quell my horrified reaction to seeing her bum literally hanging out and exposed. Haley would just laugh and wiggle the offending bottom in my face.

The filthy fingernails became a mainstay. There were so many times when I thought that Haley had been finger painting in black. She was totally unfazed and didn't care. Even Marie told me to "lighten up."

As life marched us along, Jake and I could breathe again. It was late one night when we got to bed and that damn phone rang again. When I looked at the clock it was 11 p.m. Jake grabbed it and went a whiter shade of pale.

"What?" I demanded.

"Natasha totaled her car."

OMG! OMG! OMG!

"She got a DUI, no one died, she's not hurt," Jake rattled off.

OMG!

My mind zeroed in on the good news: No one died. No one was hurt.

In crisis mode again, I felt the spotlight swing to illuminate Natasha once again. I was glad the car was totaled because I wouldn't have to argue with her about giving it back.

I knew what was coming next: mandatory AA meetings, a visit to the morgue, and loss of her license. We were back in the "fun" pool that makes you question why you ever wanted children. I vowed that remaining childless in my next life was the best idea of all.

Kids: The gift that keeps on giving.

When we finally saw our daughter, Natasha was beside herself with shame and angst. Relief flooded my system because the car was a tangled mess, but our baby girl was alive. But what had she done? Jake and I were devastated.

I drove her to court for the hearing and to sign up for community service. On the drive back to Natasha's apartment with her long-term boyfriend, she started the pity party.

She didn't want to clean up a local park. "Debmama, people are murdered in that park. It's just not safe," Natasha insisted.

"Darling, I'm sure no one is murdered between 8 a.m. and 4 p.m.," I countered, adding, "I should think that you would love making the world a more beautiful place."

She didn't love it. Instead, she bolted out of the car when we reached her destination, insisting that she didn't want any more of my "chin up" suggestions.

We couldn't "fix" Natasha any more than we could fix Haley. At least by now, I was keeping my oars to myself. She was living about an hour away now and that made it difficult for me to even see her boat or know if she was seeing the lighthouse.

Soon, I'd find out that Natasha decided not to do the community service and opted for prison time rather than make the world more beautiful. I've failed to mention until now that Haley also did prison time for a wreckage of her past having to do with the point system in California. I always told the girls, "Don't give points away for stupid offenses like not wearing your seat belt." Wearing a seat belt seemed like a no brainer.

Haley is the only person I knew who got pulled over for driving too slowly on the freeway. Maybe they could do a two-for-one in prison, my addled brain thought.

Time passed and my life went back to a version of normal including taking a commercial acting workshop with friends. Oh, that was so much fun and such a delicious therapy for a Saturday morning followed by coffee and giggles over our exploits. It was surreal watching myself on the playbacks. Who was that weird person jumping up and down with such enthusiasm?

All of this frivolity was interrupted when Natasha moved back to our area from San Diego City College after the first year, insisting she did not want to be so far away.

What could possibly go wrong?

CHAPTER TWENTY

FOUR DAYS

Natasha made it clear that coming home didn't mean living at home. Instead, she would live in town with her boyfriend, which didn't seem unusual since they had been dating since she was fifteen. Now, twenty-years-young, Natasha presented us with another shocker: This seemed to be the end of her higher educational pursuits. This wasn't up for debate. "I'm no longer a baby," she constantly reminded us. "I don't want to live with you and my Dad. I want to make my own decisions."

In light of everything, Natasha still sparkled each time I saw her. Part of me was proud that she felt so confident in her decision-making capabilities. Frankly, I had no confidence in mine.

One Saturday when I was on the way home from my acting session, Jake called me. He sounded upset. "The baby is at the house and she wants to know if she can move home to us," he posed. "She's also hysterical."

I called her. "Of course, you can move home, baby," I said.

"Always."

When I arrived at home, Natasha was still hysterical, and I noticed that she was so skinny and her face looked awful. "My boyfriend dumped me and my car is totaled," she cried. "I was fired from my job. I have no money and no home."

I was so happy that she was back. Maybe I'd just dip my oar in the water for a short period of time.

Choosing a bedroom to live in at our house since her old one was no longer available was an ordeal. She didn't like the first room offered to her. "DebMama, there's this frickin' bird who knocks his head against the window at 5 a.m.," she said.

Maybe this bird was my kindred spirit.

I went on to explain to her that the early bird catches the worm. Or maybe, he was just stopping by to say hello. Or maybe, he had really naughty kidlets and knocking his head against a window provided some relief.

Natasha didn't smile. I had a brilliant idea to hang Christmas balls outside that window. I lugged the tall ladders around and my girl was grumpy as she held the balls for me. The problem was solved. Temporarily. "The dogs like to go into the room through the doggie door and they're waking me up," she cried.

We tried bedroom number two. It was far too sunny.

Bedroom number three was gloomy, but it would do. Finally, Natasha had a new room in our house and my fairy princess was home. I just knew it would be a joyful reunion.

It didn't take long before Jake and I started to notice strange smells wafting from that room of gloom. Natasha was constantly smoking pot, which didn't seem as scary as meth to me, but I knew it wasn't good. Yet, you didn't see any crazed, adrenalized potheads. That was small comfort.

I purchased new door hardware and set about changing the knobs so she couldn't lock herself in the bedroom or bathroom. I wanted 24-7 access to Natasha's main rooms.

Meanwhile, Jake and I came up with an agreement. Pot wouldn't be allowed in the house. Natasha was also required to take a random drug test. These were our boundaries. We told her that if she couldn't quit on her own then we could explore rehab again and then sober living. In my heart, I knew she would do none of the above, move out and I'd lose another daughter. The last time almost killed me.

I couldn't believe that I'd have to do this twice.

Natasha was outraged about the fact that her privacy was invaded in this way. Too bad!

"No pot smoking here or your butt will be in rehab so fast," I reminded her. She knew that I didn't make empty threats anymore.

It wasn't long before Natasha made her decision.

She made up with her boyfriend and left our house.

I wasn't sad this time. Jake and I looked at each other relieved that our fragile sense of peace and serenity had returned when she shut that front door.

We wore our numbness like a coat of armor. We were veterans in arms, returned from some horrible war that we were unprepared to fight in the first place. We certainly weren't prepared to fight it again.

SHIFT & SHINE

THURSDAY

Then came four days that left me speechless. It was the Thursday of Thanksgiving and I decorated the table with such a feeling of joy while the savory smell of roasting turkey filled the house. My baby Natasha was coming back to enjoy the holidays with her parents as was Haley. "DebMama, let's make two different stuffing's," said my beautiful girl Natasha and I agreed that would be an amazing idea.

We had a lovely dinner together. As I gazed out at the setting sun, I allowed myself to breathe.

The girls even teased me, insisting they would like to "drop me off" at rehab in the ghetto, so I could get firsthand knowledge of what it was like to be in that environment. "Second hand is fine with me," I joked. They proceeded to laugh and tell funny stories. Some weren't so funny, and I saw Jake's eyes start to glaze over. I felt for him.

Haley even shared that when her acting teacher had told her to lose ten pounds of weight to be camera-ready, that had been her "hello, crystal meth" moment. OMG.

I did not have much time to ponder on what she had just said, other than an over whelming urge to find that teacher and strangle him.

However, it was Thanksgiving, so I pulled myself together.

Even more stuffing was coming out of the oven for snacking. Haley asked Natasha, "Can I take some to go, please?"

Natasha shook her head. "No, it's for my friends."

"Don't be so frickin' selfish," Haley said.

"Selfish!" Natasha exploded "You are a frickin' selfish bitch."

"You've put everyone through so much. You are selfish!" Haley shouted.

Natasha was shouting even louder "You put everyone through so much more. I hate you and wish I had another family!"

"I wish you had another family, too!" Haley yelled.

"I'm frickin' leaving!" Natasha responded.

"I'm frickin' leaving, too!" Haley said.

"Can I leave, too, please?" Jake begged.

How had a nice family holiday ended up in this jumbled mess? This time, they were high off their anger. They reminded me of the creatures in Jurassic Park, beautiful, batting long eyelashes, purring, gorgeous and then ..... at any given instant ....they morph into spitting, scary, biting horrors.

My girls were Raptors!

They weren't extinct at all.

Jake and I were just fresh meat each time they walked in our door.

FRIDAY

The following day, it was time for Haley's one-year sobriety lunch at the Malibu Café. I wondered if Natasha would show up given the prior nights interchange. She breezed into the restaurant. There were about eight of us including Haley's friends and students. To my amazement, it's like the raptor battle of Thanksgiving had never happened. We were back in *Alice in Wonderland*.

Natasha gave a rousing speech about her beloved sister's sobriety, and we clinked our Perrier water. In turn, Haley thanked her baby sister for her support. There were hugs all around. I marveled that the girls were so good at not holding a grudge. Perhaps, they were more evolved than I even hoped.

SATURDAY

This was Natasha's big day of getting photos taken for her new portfolio. We started early with hair and makeup and I was absolutely stunned by the transformation. She sparkled even brighter if that were possible. We set off for the location with a plan formed for me to run back and forth with clothes, shoes and moral support. I was also tasked with video-taping the entire proceedings.

The transformation was amazing as Natasha morphed into this even more beautiful creature that loved the camera. The feelings were returned because the proofs were dazzling. I felt as if I was taking a rare glimpse into her future.

The shoot ended late at night and I was on the edge of total exhaustion. Somehow, I had also ended up with a rather large bag of Natasha's stuff left in my car. My last task was carrying it to her car. Popping her trunk, I saw a huge, angled, red and round velvet bag. Suddenly, I was having this exchange with Natasha.

"OMG! I don't like to think of you doing things like that!"

Natasha went slightly red in the face, apparently thinking, "Wow, DebMama is really clued in."

She asked, "What do you think this is?"

"A butt sex lifter," I stammered. I had seen one once and it looked sort of the same to me.

Natasha nearly peed her pants laughing. Then she unzipped the pillow to reveal a huge bong! It looked like something from the Marrakesh.

Of course, she assured me the bong did not belong to her. She was merely transporting it.

"Really?" I said, deciding there was no answer that could have made me happy.

My life was officially surreal. I felt ready for the mad house; my poor tattered brain in need of repair.

I collapsed on my bed next to Jake that night.

"What's wrong?" he asked.

"My brain hurts," I replied.

SUNDAY

Oh, happy day! Jake was off to Vegas for a convention for a couple of days and I was going to have a lazy, lovely sleepy Sunday. When the phone rang, I debated whether to answer it or not.

I answered.

Haley had a very bad fall from a horse and was on her way in an ambulance to the hospital. With lightning speed, I was in my car and at the hospital for one of those "forever" waits to hear any news. Finally, the doctor appeared.

"You daughter has a punctured lung, three broken ribs and a broken back," he said. "She's hanging on by a thread."

Time stopped.

Haley was moved into the pulmonary cardiac intensive care and placed on a breathing machine. I couldn't believe this was happening. A machine was now breathing to keep my precious child alive. All alone, I gazed at my baby looking so vulnerable and small laying in that hospital bed, hooked up to equipment with tubes going into her body.

Oh, how I loved her.

Oh, why didn't I have a wishing wand to make it better?

Hours turned into days. A doctor finally told me that Haley would live and she wouldn't be crippled. Thank you, God! Her broken back consisted of splinter breaks and her spine would eventually fuse all the pieces back together again. She would need to wear a tight corset wrapped around her middle for support when she walked. She would be able to walk!

Marie assumed a frontline position next to me. She fed the horses and dogs before coming to the hospital. Gratitude washed over me. She actually would find me sitting on the floor outside of the intensive care unit. Somehow, she found me food late at night when the hospital cafeteria was closed.

Yes, Jake offered to come back from his trip early, that was such a kind offer but I told him there was nothing more to be done and to focus on his music event. "I'm okay…well, not really okay," I said.

Add another 50 years to my age.

I figured I was pushing about 150 now.

When she opened her eyes, Haley looked at me. She could talk and asked me to please stay the night. The nurse wasn't so sure because no one is normally allowed to sleep over in intensive care. Haley started to cry loudly, and the nurse acquiesced.

At night, the whole ward had a kind of a hush that was harmonized by the hum of the breathing machines. Thin curtains separated the patients from the nurse's station, and it was comforting to know that they were right there.

My poor baby slept while I watched over her. I wanted to wave that magic wand and take away her black eye that was so swollen. I wanted to fix her back. I wanted to sleep, but that was impossible.

The breathing machine gave me a weird sense of comfort and calm with its gentle whooshing in and out. That air was life.

In the middle of night, I could also hear the hushed voices of the nurses and doctors whispering to each other. An occasional loud beep from one of the beds had my arm hair standing straight up. It couldn't be good.

The nurse finally told me that my chair should collapse into a bed. It wasn't easy and I didn't realize the thing had wheels. When I tried to manipulate it, it took off with me in it, whooshing me through the curtains and parking in front of the nurse's station.

I looked up. The nurses and I shared a big smile.

The days passed in an excruciatingly slow way. I wished I could cuddle my daughter, but each time she moved a fraction, the pain was dizzying. After a week, I was told that I could bring her home to my house.

Jake knew. He didn't dare say a word.

At home, I watched her sleep, remembering that brilliant little girl who arrived in America when she was six. I remembered little Haley at the dog park, begging all the owners to just allow her to walk their dogs. She would then proudly take them for a turn around the park. Inevitably, the owners would follow her to meet me. They were so captivated by this little girl with the charming British accent.

Young Haley loved to tell me about the different breeds of dogs and their ages. We would spend hours there and sit under the sprinklers so we could have an instant cool off on a hot day. The cost? Free. The gift? Endless.

She was such a bright, captivating, sunny little person.

The first day home with us, Haley opened her eyes after a nap. I was hopping around with her pain meds and a glass of water.

"Get rid of those, Mom," she grumbled. "I won't be taking them."

I was dumbstruck.

"I won't risk my sobriety," she said. "I'm an addict. Remember?"

Oh my God. Time stood still. My gift was clarity. I could see my daughter's unshakeable determination and her very character shining through at her worst physical moment.

I was grateful for this glimpse into my daughter's soul.

The only medicine I gave her was holding her sweet face in my hands with tears running down my face.

"You know, I love you, right?" I said. "More than anything in the whole world."

The courage she showed me in the following weeks took my breath way. Haley asked me to drive her to her horses each day to check on their welfare. She told me that she needed to be a good Mom, so none of her animals would ever be taken from her again.

Eventually, Haley hobbled around in the rain to make sure those horses were fed. At night, I'd hear her sobbing into her pillow when the pain was extreme. She never took one pill. My flawed, amazing daughter was in the light and I was seeing her clearly. She was rowing her own boat.

After several weeks, Haley finally went back to her own home. I choked back tears as she drove way and resisted the overwhelming urge to make her stay with me, so I could micromanage her safety. I knew those feelings were wrong.

I had been given the heady gift of witnessing her courage. It's not a gift that I asked for, but it was there and I accepted it. Her gift was wrapped up in a bow of her pain and determination not to give in. She filled me with awe.

I witnessed her redemption.

Finally, my tears were those of happiness and gratitude.

She had shown me that her sobriety was more important to her than anything else in the world.

I wept for all mankind.

CHAPTER
TWENTY-ONE

JAKE

The girls seemed to be on the right track, so it was time to move along with our lives. There was no manual for survivors of a family war. Jake and I watched a Charlie Sheen roast one night and I commented to Jake, "I really like Charlie. I guess I like flawed people."

"Well, you've surrounded yourself with them," Jake said with a smile.

There were a few other flaws in my life. During all of this turmoil, my company had gone bankrupt. I was devastated, but I had been unable to keep it all together when the stock market fell apart in 2007. Work was off my plate and I got to exhale for the first time in many years of circling the sun.

Over time, Jake and I had a newfound gentleness with each other. We assumed a rhythm to our lives as true empty nesters. Our home truly was our sanctuary and I felt peace and serenity there for the first time in years. I dug and dug some more and flowers were shooting up everywhere.

Something was still off.

I could feel Jake's light starting to dim a little inside his lampshade. I loved him so much and felt if I could just come up with the right project, I could reengage him in his own life. His brilliance, tenacity, and creative skills would shine right back through him again for a midlife rebirth.

I felt inspired to come up with reality shows. I had such amazing material with the humans I knew and felt with the cast of characters in my life, I was in the middle of a show that was a cross between The *Beverly Hillbillies* and *Green Acres*.

In short order, I learned how to write a treatment, register it, and what a sizzle reel was when it came to pitching new material to the powerhouses in Hollywood. *Malibu Horsewives, Man's Fattest Friend, Love on a Plate*. On and on, my brain went.

I reached out and "pitched" the idea for the show to an old friend, Kenny, who had originally introduced Jake and me. He loved it and raised money for the sizzle reel to be shot. My girlfriends and I had so much fun. If my friends resisted, I assured them the worst thing that could happen was we would have three minutes of video of us to watch when we were old ladies!

It missed the mark and turned into a tame version of the *Real Housewives* franchise. None of us wanted to pretend to be nasty. It was still fun to try and we had a lot of meetings about it. Jake seemed to have the old glimmer back in his eyes.

One major change was when we decided to put our beloved home up for sale. We received an all cash offer within two days, it would enable us to buy another smaller ranch free and clear.

Jake sat with me the next day.

"Babe, I just can't leave here," he said. "I love it too much." I took a deep inhale and replied, "Okay, my darling. We shall figure something out."

I hated to see him in any anguish.

A couple of years later and it was no longer a question of whether or not to sell our beloved home. It was a short sale born out of the economy and necessity.

I tried to put on a happy face. "Don't worry, darling," I gently told Jake. "Let's go and lease a house on the beach. It will be a new start."

"Yep," Jake replied. "A ranch would feel like a sideways move and we wouldn't own it."

"We shall make this fun," I promised. "You always had the horses and the garden for me. Let's do this one for you."

I located an area on the beach, further north and less expensive. Meanwhile, the chap who had purchased our home went back on his word to let us rent back and wanted us out immediately. A few days before Thanksgiving, men were packing, groaning and moving all of our stuff. We went from 4,500 to 3,200 square feet. I started giving away treasures. There was no time to miss them.

Thanksgiving was becoming a catalyst in my memory banks.

I told myself I was an excelled un-packer. My friends will attest that in three days, I can have any home straight and organized. Little did I know how much I would need this skill set. Jake was quite the opposite. He did not like moving and I could feel him wanting to climb out of his skin at the thought of this major life changer.

The new house was three stories high and actually built like a bunker. I just wanted to have a front door on the beach – and we did for the first time in our lives. We had a lovely room to watch golden sunsets, but instead of making it a romantic spot, Jake put his giant TV in there.

So much for romance.

After we moved, Jake sat in the top living room where you could watch the most wonderful sunsets. He wanted no part of nature's wonders and pulled the curtains tightly, so the TV wasn't affected. I used to teasingly tell him when he transcended someday, I was going to bury him in that TV with a bottle of decent red wine.

I noticed he was no longer able to walk without wobbling.

He was crumbling both mentally and physically – and I needed to fortify him again.

It was November and we were living at the beach. Poor Jake was depressed and not interested in a huge storm that was coming in. I found the weather exciting. Jake was more concerned with our flooded garage and his prized possession, his car, surrounded by water.

Our street was closed off, no one could leave the area and the cherry on his cake that day was that the evening news showed our actual block on the television set Jake was watching. It made it even more official that we were underwater when we saw it on TV. Jake muttered, "I knew we should have never moved to the ocean."

We agreed to take turns walking the dogs on the beach. I thought it would be good for him. He would re-engage, love life and become happy again. As usual, I had it all figured out. Why keep my oars in my boat? I could certainly row for my husband while watching out for waves that could drown both of us.

As it turned out, Jake didn't want to walk the dogs as he was unsteady on his feet by now, plus he hated the weather. It was too windy, too cold and too rainy. So, I walked them, and he was right about the wind. Gale force gusts almost knocked me over while sheets of sand hurt as they were hurled in my face. I got one of those funny Balaclava headgear units to wear. I thought I was definitely in Scotland on the coldest, bleakest beach. I did get some funny pictures to post on Facebook.

One day, my little Terrier Jack ran way down the beach chasing a seagull. He went further, further, further away from me and suddenly it looked like he was a mile away. I was screaming at the top of my lungs, "Jaaaaacccccckkkkkk!" My voice bounced back to me on the wind when a huge wave picked him up. I ran and ran, screaming as I raced towards the water.

I was so grateful when the wave spat him out.

Jack marked another black mark when it came to the beach experience.

Eventually, the days evened out and we began to settle. I met people as I trundled up and down the beach with my dogs and I collected the most beautiful, sparkling rocks as my treasures.

Each day, Jake would pop his nose out from the top balcony and wave to me. Then he would disappear back into the darkened room that became his cave, headquarters and place of existence.

Spring came around, beautiful and full of promise, and the seals on the beach arrived to play. I was delighted. A few days later, I learned that they were baby seals and were malnourished and dying. That blew my mind, so I frantically called the wildlife people and tried to help them rescue these precious creatures.

OK, I had to give it to Jake. Maybe the beach was no fun.

"There is just too much sand," Jake said. "And too many strange humans lurking around."

I promised him that we would move. I would find something he liked better that didn't included starving and helpless animals and monster storms.

Did he fancy something that looked like Venice? How about an area back from the beach that was on a canal? Would that work?

"Yes, let's look, Deb," he said. Five months into house number one, I found myself getting reacquainted with those moving boxes again. Overwhelmed? Yes. But I worked feverishly to make Jake happy.

"Oh, come away with me, my love. Let's move to the channels. I know for sure you will be happy there," I said. "Please, please come away with me. No sand to blow in your precious face. No unknown humans making you feel uncomfortable in your lampshade. No me freaking out about dead seals."

"I will unpack super quickly," I promised. "You will feel no discomfort. Please let's replant you. I know you will grow strong and come back to me. Please. Please. I love you sooooo much. Let's just try a new garden under our feet."

From 3,500 square feet, we went down to 2,800 square feet. It was no big deal. I'd just keep giving things away. I would walk towards my daughters who were enlisted to help me with these many moves. I'd call this time: The Year of Moving Dangerously.

I had a saucepan, frying pan, clothes, vases and friends to help move them, although Marie and Devora insisted I was quickly using up all my moving chips. I owed them big time forever and ever.

After we moved again to the Venice Canal, I told Jake we should join the local sailing club and make new friends. It was just the two of us now and there was so much fun to be had as a couple with no responsibilities.

"No, baby," he replied. "I just don't feel up to it."

I hired a personal trainer for both of us because my man had always worked out. Jake gamely tried for a couple of months, but told me it was just not working for him. His stance was becoming increasingly wobbly. Worried, I booked doctor appointments for him to finally find out what was wrong.

The first night at our Venice home, I saw the most amazing sight through the back window. I kid you not, but the ship Proud Mary was steaming right by the back window going down the channel. I was so excited I started jumping up and down and threw up the curtains. I screamed and ran outside to the garden where I started waving to everyone. "I see you! Do you see me!" I cried.

It was 15 minutes of pure delight.

Coming in, I felt light and happy. My man sat down next to me.

"Deb, I really don't like that. We need to keep the curtains closed. I feel my privacy is being invaded."

My heart began to pound softly.

"Okay, baby, okay," I said.

My girlfriends, my amazing earth angels, all came to visit me and marveled at how well our "stuff" actually fit into so many different homes. Some joked that maybe I should start an unpacking company.

Maybe I could.

I was ready for anything.

The back garden went down to the dock and I had visions of us sailing off it, having adventures. Natasha and her boyfriend did just that. They went out in two canoes on the fourth of July with me encouraging them not to be scared of the big yachts out there and giving them little flashlights to find their way back. Oh, they had such a fun adventure and I was so happy.

The following morning some new neighbors appeared at our dock on their stand-up paddleboards. Super nice humans, they had come to make friends with us. "Would you like to come paddle board with us?" they asked.

Jake said, "No thanks." He could not think of one activity he would rather do less.

I thought, "What the heck."

My answer to their offer: "Yes, sure."

I was fully clothed, hair and makeup done, but I could stand up on that wobbly thing, right?

I stepped on with confidence. I think I made two strokes out to sea and then splash! I promptly fell into the water. Wet clothes really weigh a lot. They assured me I would improve, as there was no other choice really. I thanked them for the experience.

A couple of days later and I took Natasha to "have a go" at stand-up paddle boarding. This time I was prepared and wore my bathing suit. Natasha was a natural, paddling all around the island and looking like a beautiful fairy with her long flowing hair drifting around her head in the light sea winds. She looked as if she had been born to this activity.

I wobbled, fell, and clambered back on. I was super relieved when it was over.

However, there were no steps to climb up from the water to get out and I didn't have the body strength to pull myself up onto the dock.

I panicked.

Natasha pulled at me, but she is petite, I was a beached drowning whale and made it unintentionally hard for her to help.

"Deb, stop struggling," she said. "You frighten me when you make that funny face."

I was sure I was about to drown, but eventually Natasha managed to pull me up and out.

"Deb, next time do a couple of tequila shots. I have never seen anyone so rigid," she laughingly teased me. "How do you stay on your horse?"

Lots of superglue on my bottom, I thought.

Weeks passed and I was still in pain for Jake who was checked out.

"My love, you still seem so sad. What pains you? How can I help you? You feel isolated here, yes?" I asked.

My new solution was to move closer to Malibu/Calabasas. He could go for meetings in Hollywood and feel like himself again.

"I am sooooo beyond sorry this second transplant of a home is not going well for you, I feel like you are ebbing away from me every day," I told him.

I personally call our bodies our lampshades, which we choose to decorate in various ways. Inside the lampshade is the all-important light bulb, the light of our life. Jake's was still growing dimmer and dimmer.

Marie and I noticed Jake's health decline, and very, very quickly. He had all the signs of Parkinson's disease, shuffling rather than walking, losing all motor skills, the Parkinson's mask of the drooped face and becoming incontinent. Jake was too proud a man to ever allow a doctor to confirm our diagnosis even though I begged him to see a specialist.

"Jake, please come back to me, please," I implored. "This is supposed to be our fun years. No kidlets. Just us and our dogs. Please come back to me. Turn up your light bulb. I need you and miss you, my soul mate. Please come back. I will turn myself inside out for your happiness. Please just tell me what to do? I shall pour unending happiness into your bucket, but baby, I need you to help me.

"But, you have to put a bottom in the bucket yourself, for this to work, otherwise all the happiness I pour in just falls out" I whispered.

"My darling, I have found a new spot," I told Jake. "It's smaller, but close to Marie. We can put the horses at her ranch. And you can arrange for our projects in town."

Jake agreed and we moved. Again. We were off to the next adventure – our fourth bedroom to sleep in during a period of only eighteen months.

At the same time, my beloved Sampson was having lameness issues. I tried steroid shots and everything else to "cure" the other major love in my life. It dawned on me that my love for Sampson and Jake was unending. I was so honored to have both in my life.

Jake was having his own issues. He could no longer play the guitar and continued to wobble when he walked. Natasha realized it also when she told me, "Dad seems unsafe to drive with these days. I don't want to go in the car with him anymore."

"I know, darling," I told her. "It's so strange."

Jake went through a battery of tests to no avail. My love hadn't been able to play his beloved guitar for five years now and had an unsuccessful carpel tunnel operation along with a blood clot in his leg.

I could sense his depression. Oh, my darling man. Please just tell me what I can do to make you feel better. Please.

Jake was blunt. "I hate this new place. It's 110 frickin' degrees here!"

The heat was oppressive in the desert, but what could we do? We were settled for now and I even hung out my real estate license.

I asked Jake to help out around the house while I showed clients prospective homes. "Deb, I can't feed the dogs. I don't know how to do it," Jake insisted.

"Baby, really?" I said.

I had an opportunity to get my equine therapy certification around this time and I knew Jake wouldn't want me to launch another project. My inner assertiveness appeared because I really wanted this in my life. I read a book by Doreen Virtue and highlighted the appropriate passages. With a fast beating heart, I asked Jake to sit down and then read the passages to him. My heart pounded so fast, I felt sick.

What if he said no to my dream?

"Sounds like you already have your mind made up," he said.

I sat with it. I felt like a grown up. This wasn't about the kids or my husband.

I made a choice for myself.

I came home one day to find my husband sitting in a chair watching endless TV shows in the middle of the day. He was nodding off to sleep. It pained me to see the light within him fading to black. He brightened when Natasha came back to stay with us for the last few months before we left that house.

I was so happy to have my baby back home again and glad she could spend time with her father.

One night, she asked me the million-dollar question.

"Debmama, where did Dad go?"

"I don't know baby," I told her. "But I sure wish he would come back."

Sitting in front of the TV on an unspectacular Sunday night, my husband asked, "Deb, do you know how to open the safe?"

I felt surprised. "No, but who cares, I have you to protect me."

We didn't just have valuables in the safe. We had a gun in there in case of a break in.

"You would never forget me…would you?" Jake asked.

I thought he was nuts.

"You're sitting right here next to me. I love you. How would I ever forget you?" I said.

That Monday morning, I woke to a light kiss on my lips. It was a butterfly kiss. It was the first time Jake had ever woken me up that way and I really liked it. I wanted to tell him, but he left the room too quickly.

As I woke in the bed by gently stretching, I heard the explosion and it took me a few moments.

BANG!

Maybe the air-conditioner or something mechanical in the house had exploded.

I ran down the passageway to Jake's office and …nothing.

Entering the room, I glanced at the walk-in closet area.

Freakin blood. Everywhere!

A scream ripped from my throat!

"No!" No! No, no, no, no, no, no!

Somehow, I dialed 911.

Somehow, I stood while shock too over my entire body.

Numb, I gazed into the eyes of my beloved. They had never looked so beautiful and peaceful.

Come back, come back, come back…please don't leave me. Please baby, come back. Please, I can make it better.

My oars are ready.

In short order, the house was overrun with police while I sat in the corner of Jake's office, shaking and trembling.

Then it dawned on me. Was anyone else in the house?

OMG! I wasn't sure if Natasha had come home late.

Racing outside, I looked in the driveway and my darling baby girl's car was there. Fuck! I wanted to go to her room and wake her, but the police wouldn't let me. My poor baby was rudely ousted from her bed and strangers told her the tragic news that her father was dead. I knew Jake would never want to cause Natasha any pain. If only he had known she was home.

Where was my backward machine?

I called Devora and Marie who both came immediately to my side. My Earth Angels were on call 24-7. Devora arranged for a HAZMAT team to come and clean the room where my beloved had transcended.

I was in absolute disbelief. This is not my life. It couldn't be my life. I was in the middle of some nightmare. Any minute, I would wake up.

Oh baby, why? I loved you. Love you so much. Please come back to me. I need just one more butterfly kiss.

Somewhere a voice replied, "It's just the blink of an eye, Deb. We will be together someday."

Oh Jake. Was there something I did or did not do that caused it?

Reality flooded my senses because there were things to do.

Jake was Jewish, so we needed to have the memorial quickly. Some disembodied voice reminded me of Jewish law.

Funny, what you think of when you're in shock.

More Earth Angels arrived to organize, call and even offer to pay for the reception. My amazing Natasha pulled herself together to put together a video tribute to her father that would leave no dry eye. I didn't have time to fall apart because there was a memorial to plan and we collectively decided it would be at sunset on the beach. I was numb, so broken and dead inside.

Devora arranged for a guitarist to greet the guests while Marie organized the guest list. Victoria printed out the words of a song Jake had written for me; Claire hosted the reception. Over 150 people gathered to say goodbye.

We spoke of my husband as the sun burned pink and slowly dipped low into the ocean. It felt otherworldly.

I had arranged for a Jewish cantor to conduct the actual ceremony and he sang such lovely, spiritual songs. Towards the end of one song, the microphone went dead. The crowd chuckled. That was such a Jake move. It was like he was directing the proceedings. I could hear my Jake saying, "Cut! Enough of this shit!"

My stepson gave wonderful speeches, as did Haley and Natasha. It was Natasha who decided to do a paddle out with her friends. The waves were beyond huge that night and I wondered if a lifeguard would need to go out and rescue them, but they were fine. Someone was watching over them.

One of Natasha's friends gave me an expensive bottle of wine – the "good stuff" – before the service began. I went looking for it after the ceremony, but Natasha smiled. Her friends had chugged it before the paddle out to keep them warm.

And then it was over. Really, really over.

I went home.

The following night I couldn't sleep despite the fact that I was bone aching tired. Natasha was so amazing to me. We collapsed on the bed together, numb and numer. "Deb, let's go to the moonlight walk, let's be spontaneous!" she said. I remember pondering for all of two seconds. "Ok, baby, let's go," I said.

We walked the labyrinth; we blessed the earth and all humans.

We were on the top of the tallest mountain where you could see all of Los Angeles spread out below us. It was all twinkling back. The moon was full and about to burst. I smiled gently. My man always told me the moon pulled on his head and made him feel insane.

Oh, my man, I hope you are feeling sweet relief now.

The absolute chaos one enters into after someone transitions unexpectedly with suicide is unlike any other death. In the weeks that followed and months, I lost weight because I felt so damn numb and hollow. I went through the daily motions, but my brain seemed to be in a huge fog. I couldn't even answer the easiest of questions.

No, I didn't know the password for turning his cell phone off. It was like some surreal puzzle with people on the other end of the phone who would not budge. There was a protocol. Unless I could spit out the magic password, I couldn't cancel his account.

Being inside the house made my head throb. There were

unending piles of paperwork that seemed insurmountable. Each day, I'd try to take a little bite out of them only to add more envelopes that came in the mail. Suddenly, I was getting late notices. Was it possible that he had decided not to mail our bills in on the first of the month?

There was the morning when my landlord of our new rental house called. He was a nasty, sweaty little man with beady eyes and a huge ego. I agreed to give him a duplicate rent check delivered by my girlfriend Devora. Somehow, my Type A brain was able to call the bank and put a stop payment on the "lost" check.

I had no choice but do what Jake did. I reconciled the bank statements, paid the electric, gas and rent. These were activities that I really didn't want to do. A desert island would have been preferable, so I could plant myself face down on the earth and sob unending tears for Jake.

So, I could sob for myself.

I wrote to Jake in my journal. "Baby, Jake, please, please stop fading away from me. I am soooo scared without you. I am intrinsically a part of you. You are so noble, so good and a man of such integrity. I see all your amazing qualities so clearly. You are my love. Please, please don't leave me."

"Tears – unrelenting – are flowing down my face, Jake. Can you feel them? How can I stay here on earth without you? Please, please stay. I can't wait for the next life to see you. Will you come back to me now? As flawed as I am will you return? I miss you.

I miss us."

The business of life continued, and I gave six-week notice to my nasty little landlord. I absolutely could not sleep in that house because even that air inside of it felt toxic. Natasha moved one of her homeless friends in. She was a drug addict with a filthy mattress and two bags full of grubby stuff. My heart ached for the young girl, but I could not have her here while I was showing the house to potential tenants.

Please, universe. No more drama. No more chaos.

The landlord agreed that I could get out of the lease early, if I could find a potential new renter. Devora listed the property and I started showing it. He rejected every applicant, but I got to meet some super cool people, a necessary distraction. Even worse was when he decided to sue me for Jake's suicide. I even received harassing phone calls from the landlord's attorney and nasty emails.

I always thought that humans were basically good. Most were. Some not.

During this time, my doctor offered tranquilizers and I did a bit of better living through chemistry. My attitude towards the lawsuit: Fuck him. Let him sue me.

It would also turn out that almost six months to the day after I had written the replacement rent check and cancelled the lost check, the mf-er put the lost check through my bank. My eyes popped wide open when I reconciled my bank statement. It was just stress and more stress. All my checks bounced, and my helpful banker said the landlord knew what he was doing by waiting but he made a mistake of paying it in one day too early before the six-month expiration of "do not pay." The money was returned to me. Thank God for small miracles.

Marie was as ever extremely helpful to me during this time and obtained a copy of the coroner's report. Yes, it was ruled a suicide by gunshot. She helped me fill out all the forms needed for the death certificate. She drove me to get the final certificates and I slipped while thanking her. "Thank you, my darling for getting the gift certificates with me," I said.

It was the first time I laughed since Jake died. It felt so good just to giggle.

Suddenly, my phone started blaring out that one particular "because I'm happy" song as my ringtone. I had removed my old ringtone after Jake transitioned. Shit, shit, shit. How could I turn it off? It played three times on a loop with me pushing every button I could find to shut it up. It went through three repeats of "Over the Horizon." I never downloaded that song.

If Marie hadn't been with me to witness this, I swear I would have thought I was totally insane.

Of course, it was Jake communicating with us. I remembered something I read about the dead communicating through airwave frequencies because it's all energy. As soon as we burst through Marie's door, she Googled, Over the Horizon. We couldn't believe our eyes when the most beautiful video with that melody began to play. The video looked like a scene from heaven with waterfalls and snowcapped mountains. The majesty of it took my breath away.

There were also written words scrolling under the video that spoke of there being a huge rising up of Rainbow Warriors. I felt stunned, Jake was letting us know he was happy and at one with the Universe. It was such a comfort and I felt such gratitude. Suddenly, I felt a sense of purpose. I could be a rainbow warrior on this side.

Time passed and I found solace driving Jake's car. I felt so close to him and even listened to the Over the Horizon song on the radio. When it came on unexpectedly, I wasn't scared, but said, "Hey, my man. I hear you."

I felt thankful.

It wasn't easy adjusting no matter how many signs I was given. One day, I went to an engagement party on my own and chatted with everyone. At some point towards the end, I felt so utterly lonely. It was no wonder because I was so used to my man standing somewhere and always watching me. He was the one who usually said, 'Baby, it's time to go home now. You look so beautiful. I love you."

There were more tears that day when I climbed into his car by myself. I felt bleak and empty, so I cranked up the radio …and the song played again. Chills swept over me as I shouted the words from my open-air car with the wind rushing through my hair and tears stinging my eyes. Thank you, my man. Thank you. I love you so much. Keep talking to me.

Living alone hit me hard. We had so much stuff that had accumulated from years of living. I put up a post on Facebook offering most of it for free. I gave away brand new sofas and tables. Where could I move all this stuff, anyway? The task of moving yet again and by myself was actually overwhelming and Marie came to sort through the endless paperwork with me.

It turns out that Natasha was pretty mad at me because I asked her friend to leave. I just couldn't take the chaos from this girl or her black plastic bags of stuff that reminded me of perilous days with Haley. Even Natasha's anger couldn't get a reaction from me now. I was numb and operating on little sleep thanks to the monsters that came into my head at night.

Even trying to go to sleep brought fever dreams where Jake was still alive. It felt so vivid and real that I'd open my tired, swollen eyes and the first thing I could focus on was my hands shaking. One blink and the reality hit me. He was gone. The dreams were in the past and I was losing Jake again and again.

For a short time, I decided to live on the sofas of friends who accepted this bag lady with two dogs in tow. I felt ragged and disorientated as I moved around and I'm sure I also looked pretty darn scary. Marie kept reminding me to shower and eat. My poor dogs, Jack and Snoopy, tried to be comforts, but their lives were also turned upside down.

Finally, I put an ad in the local paper. Wanted: Guest House. I'm happy to help with gardening, animals and humans. I was feeling the gentle energy to move near the life-affirming ocean. I even opened a post office box near where I wanted to live in Malibu because I still believed that the power of intention was indeed powerful.

It wasn't long before I was in Malibu Canyon looking at a guesthouse and meeting the owners. I walked through the garden that led to this tiny house and I was absolutely entranced. It was a sacred spot, perched halfway up a cliff with panoramic ocean views. Butterflies danced around my head as I moved, and I could hear the parrots of Malibu calling to each other. A flock of fifty flew right over me!

My weary eyes gazed at the grounds while the owners explained that the house had two meditation areas of goddesses. "One of the goddesses cries unending tears for the world," I was told. "She will not return to the source herself until every human experiencing any kind of suffering has been returned to source/heaven."

Goosebumps began to rise on my arm and I silently thanked Jake for helping me find some peace. I could actually feel his energy guiding me towards this sacred place.

The couple that owned the house was also a breath of fresh air. They were around 80 years young, but sparkled to the point I could feel the goodness coming from their souls. I fell in love.

216

Jane was the wife and said, "Well, we can't agree to anything until we interview your dogs!"

I promised to bring the dogs the following day, knowing they were perfect because I loved them to the moon and back. My Jack Russell and Beagle Basset Hound sat quietly through the interview like perfect dogs. I was about to sign the lease when the hound named Snoopy spotted a dog down below and started howling as only that breed can. The volume seemed to rise with each second.

The owners just smiled and handed me the lease to sign.

Phew!

It turns out that Jane was the medicine I needed. I just wanted to drink her in and absorb her knowingness, kindness and then borrow a few of her secrets of life. The best part was that I wasn't couch surfing any longer and my dogs had a garden. I felt the need to do a happy, relieved dance each time my toes touched the ocean. Jane told me that Jake had definitely guided me to them.

"This is the perfect spot to grieve," she said.

Was it clearing out the old house? Or was it moving to a new spot? I don't know what moved the old energy or brought in a new source. I operated from a place called "no other choice."

My new little home was soon filled with my packing boxes that went from one end of the structure to the other. I called that house "my little train" because it was long and thin, but also white, clean and modern. It wasn't a match in size for my stuff but felt so cozy to me. I had a bed with sheets to call my own. Woooohooo!

My girlfriend Michelle visited and told me, "Deb, you are now a gypsy fairy. We must move everything out of this space that does not give you joy."

We huffed and puffed and soon the outside was filled with boxes that in my prior life contained things I considered treasures. Michelle even moved the dining room table around into a spot I never would have thought of in a million years.

"Does this speak to you?" she asked, holding up various things.

Whoosh! The things that didn't speak to me were gone.

When I looked around, my train was transformed into what I can only describe as an art gallery with my favorite paintings leaning on the walls. My statues were all placed with love and looked as if they had been custom-made for this exact location.

Marie had the idea to place the sofa on cinder blocks, so I could see the sunrise and sunset from this elevated place. I lugged all 20 of those blocks down a 500-foot winding and quite steep staircase and back to my train. Each brick represented a labor of love, plus it was a hell of an arm workout.

Oh my God.

This place.

This would be the train to heaven.

Soon, I hung my hummingbird feeders and about fifty birds were whirling around my head making their comforting little beeps. I could also see them clearly from my sofa. It was such a magical and amazing place for healing.

My dogs and I exhaled.

Isolated from everyone, I'd wait for the magic time of five o'clock to roll around, so I could open a bottle of wine and medicate.

And so, my year of being underwater began. Well-meaning friends would call me and say, "So and so couldn't get out of bed for two years after her husband died." Well, guess what? Neither could I. But I didn't know it was a competition. Gently, I would reply, "Really…gosh, I'm so sad for her."

I considered the well-meaning friend on the other end of the phone and chose not to share my gut searing pain. In the future I would begin seeing a therapist named Marilyn who would help me get rid of this type of "mis-thinking."

In August, Jake committed suicide and by mid-September, I moved into the Malibu train. By November, I had to put my beloved Sampson to sleep.

I felt like a bad country song.

One day, I approached Sampson in the field and knew he could no longer walk over to me for a treat. I made the hardest phone call to my vet. "It's time," I simply said.

On that Monday morning before Thanksgiving, my group gathered at 9 a.m. It was Marie, Ava and I. Sampson walked majestically out to the grassy green area.

"Be brave, Deb," I told myself. "He needs your courage."

"It will be fine, Sam," I said. "You will be in heaven, soon."

I wanted to howl at the moon, shred my clothes, cut off my hair or amputate a body part. Grief coursed through every fiber of my being – unending, unbending, unforgiving grief. Every wound was open.

After, I morphed into what I can only describe as a zombie. I was frozen, jagged, raged pain on two legs. At five each day, I used the taste of sweet wine to numb me. Wine was my solace, my new love.

My two little dogs were the only things that could get me out of bed in the morning. I'd feed them and walk them. I adored those happy little faces staring up at me. Then I would return to my haven and stare at the ceiling for hours and hours.

Where had my vibrant-self gone?

Answer: She was dead to me.

I was informed that I needed to make pilgrimages to see various family members. I felt sooo tired. I really didn't think I had the energy to make these visits. My first stop was Seattle where I saw my stepson Jason and it was a good visit. Then it was off to Northern California to see Haley, my St. Francis of Assisi in high heels. She was so overjoyed to see me and the feeling was mutual.

The two-hour ride back to her ranch at a steady 80 miles per hour into the middle of nowhere was like medicine. Haley now lived on ten beautiful acres with twenty horses, fifty peacocks, seven cats, one goat, and one duck named Affleck, plus two bulls, two cows and five alpacas. Did I mention the five dogs and eight pot-bellied pigs that lived inside?

The outside was meticulously kept. My smile went wide.

"Yes, Mom," she said. "This keeps me sober."

Oh my God, child. Whatever keeps you sane is all I can wish for as your mother.

Haley was in a state of agitation. Her favorite pot-bellied pig, Spike, whom she had raised from six weeks and was now five years old, was missing. I felt a wave of guilt as she had been away for so long collecting me from the airport. She began to make frantic calls down a list of neighbors. "Yes, he is black and white," she said. "Super friendly."

She learned one of the neighbors was particularly trigger-happy. She called him and the wife answered. "Yes, my husband did shoot a pig last night. He thought it was a wild boar," she said.

I could hear the frustration in my daughter's voice. She went on at length to explain the difference between a wild boar and a pot-bellied pig. The wife replied, 'Well, it's too late. We already dropped him at the butchers and had him sliced up."

My mouth dropped open and I heard Haley say, "Well, I wouldn't eat him if I were you. He had bucolic plague. If you eat him, you will be severely sick."

Bravo, my child, bravo.

When she hung up, gut wrenching, body shaking sobs left her poor heart. "I loved him, Mom. I really loved him. He was my baby!"

Later that day, a truck pulled up at Haley's ranch and scary looking people piled out of the car. Some were missing teeth; others were wearing suspenders. They were shouting and honking the horn. "Where's the owner?" they barked. Haley was far away at the end of her ranch feeding her horses. She couldn't hear them.

With hatred in my heart and scorn, I marched towards them, wishing I had a double-barreled shotgun.

"Who wants to know?" I barked.

Yes, I knew I was in Deliverance country.

These dreadful humans confirmed that it was indeed Spike that they had shot, killed and taken to be carved up.

Haley was in unspeakable pain for the remainder of my visit.

I had a brilliant idea.

"Darling, let's go to the hardware store and get orange paint, animal friendly paint. We can paint your phone number on the sides of your potbellies. Hunters will know they're pets," I said.

Hardware visit complete, bright orange paint on hand, we started to paint the piggies. They squirmed and squealed their objections. It was actually a pretty funny sight as I watched Haley rolling around on the floor, determined to paint the phone number on.

Ever helpful, I held the pot of orange paint. Somehow, it eventually popped out of my hands and went whooshing through the air. I felt as if I was watching in slow motion. Everything, and I do mean everything, in the kitchen was now aglow with huge pools of bright orange, sticky paint.

Haley – who was married now – had a lovely husband who suggested that perhaps I should just sit on the couch and watch.

An amazing fit of giggles came over me – the first since Jake's death. I could not stop. The more I tried to push the giggles back down, the worse it got. I couldn't catch my breath. Haley was beside me, gently wrapping her arms around me. She started giggling, too.

Oh, the absurdity of it all.

Oh, the joy of giggles.

Back in Malibu, I was in my train that was perched halfway up a mountain. Soon it would be Christmas and I decided that Natasha and I would go to the United Kingdom. It would be a trip that would revolve around museums, pubs, green countryside and family.

Natasha and I boarded the plane and we were so very excited. We were on Virgin Airlines and with my foggy brain I had booked the tickets online. Apparently, I hadn't paid very much attention to detail. Natasha and I boarded and walked further and further to the back of the plane. We were almost at the rear entrance and looked at each other with a sort of "whoa" vibe. Our seats were in front of the toilet and didn't recline.

Thank God, Natasha has a great sense of humor. We spent the trip totally entangled in each other's limbs. Note to self: Look at the seat placement before you push the purchase button.

MEDITATION

I had always attended a monthly chant, singing meditation given by the super talented Stella Davis. It felt so comforting to have her amazing voice fill the room, as we would sing various God source praises from all religions. I loved the sounds of the sitar filling that room.

I noticed an email from her offering a course in Reiki Training and felt compelled to sign up. I wanted to be a conduit, so I studied and received my Reiki master practitioner certificate.

Suddenly, I felt so filled with source energy because I did have a healing force coming through me.

Stella mentioned that I was particularly open because of my loss. She even saw Jake standing beside me when I went through the blessing initiation process. Stella said he was tightly bound to the earth and unable to move on because of my immense grief.

I decided to have a cutting ceremony where his spirit would be released. I even mentioned this to Natasha who in no short order told me, "Debmama, if Dad wants to stay here, let him. Why would you let him go?"

There would be no cutting ceremony.

Around the same time, I interviewed for a job as a part time dog walker. Natasha weighed in again. "Deb, what are you doing?" she asked. "People should be walking your dogs." I appreciated her input, but felt as if dog walking would be a gift to me. On the interview, I was told I needed to be "invisible" on collecting the pooches if the people were home. Yes, well, that would not be a problem.

I felt invisible.

What to do with my other days? I reached out to an equine therapist who worked at Big Heart Ranch in Malibu and asked to volunteer. Cori was love on two legs, an irreverent tomboy, and took me in with open arms. I grew so attached to the endless stream of fragile, broken but still strong humans, all of them in different Malibu rehabs.

I got so much more than I gave.

One day, Cori asked me to build something with the horse equipment that was scattered around the field. Suddenly, I became a participant in this therapy. "What should I build?" I pondered.

Inspiration came my way. I placed a muck bucket under the shade of the majestic oak tree. I laid a rope around in a square. I placed the horse in front of my square. I took the rake and held it up in my hand, inside of the rope boundary.

"OK, Deb," Cori asked me. "What does it mean?"

"Well, Jake is the muck bucket. I have placed him beneath the shady limbs of the oak," I said. "The ropes are my chariots. I am holding my sword or rake high above my head. I am Boudicca, queen of the chariots, ready for battle with my big girl pants on – solidly."

Equine therapy. It works.

I spoke with a client about how valued and loved he was in his life. He tried to kill himself the prior week.

I was waking up.

Slowly. Slowly.

Valentine's Day came with no flowers or card for me. I decided to try and be proactive. I took myself to a local junk store that benefitted the homeless. "Jake, Sampson, please show me a treasure," I said. Almost immediately, I stumbled over to an old tatty chandelier that cost fifteen dollars.

"Thank you," I whispered under my breath.

I would restore this treasure, so I set about getting new crystals. Joyfully, I hung that chandelier dead center over my window overlooking the ocean in my new home. I did a happy dance on that Valentine's Day. I felt giddy when the sun caught the crystals making my room look like it was filled with pink and white stars.

To this day, it hangs beside my bed. It's a gift from my beloveds.

Humans show up in unexpected earth angel roles and looking back you just can't imagine how you could have survived the drowning you were experiencing without them. They literally put their whole body down to physically yank you back up to take a gulp of air…sputter, cough, sputter, breath, breath.

One such earth angel was my friend named Devora: Type-A, take charge, super woman extraordinaire.

She was the one I could call at one a.m., two a.m. or three a.m. sobbing that my pain was just too much to live through. On the other end of the phone line came that loving voice. "It's okay, Deb," she would say. "Feel your pain. Keep breathing. We need you here. It's not your time yet."

I felt unattached to the earth, totally and utterly disconnected.

I would take my little family, my two dogs and I, over to her ranch. I'd feel such peace sitting in one of her perfectly staged vignettes or a gathering of chairs under an oak tree. Or perhaps it would be a few chairs on the front porch. I knew the place would make the most beautiful bed and breakfast. I felt that I had been magically transported to the middle of Italy with her olive trees gracing the sky.

Devora was remodeling the main house, so she was living in the guesthouse. It was such a beautiful space with high ceilings and a lot of fabulous light streaming in. Devora decided to take her prior therapy training and use it on me. She encouraged me to write each morning. "Don't let your pen leave the paper. Just get it all out," she said.

My early work looked like this:

> *Stunned, stunned, stunned --- lonely, lonely, lonely*
> *sooooooo frickin' confused*
> *bitter, bitter, bitter*
> *hapless helpless*
> *disgust at myself, disgusted*
> *I am stupid, stupid, stupid,*
> *low energy low energy*
> *flat lining flat lining*
> *---fuck, fuck, fuck --- bloody hell, silly girl, silly girl...Its*
> *ok, it's gonna be ok.*

This was one days emoting.
Then came the next.

I am soooo sick of myself being so fucking sad.

The pain inside is debilitating, if anyone can see me, my limbs are severed off, gushing blood.

I am so fed up pretending I don't hurt.

I miss you both so much.

I miss the threads of my life

I miss my purpose

Jake, I loved and love you

Sam, I loved and love you.

I hurt.

I am sorry

I want to come and find you both

What will stop this gaping wound of my cracked open heart, throbbing with each involuntary breath? I don't want to feel guilty.

I feel like a need a cancer cut out of myself.

I miss my brain.

I don't like this thick fog

I want to help other humans.

I need to do the work and help myself.

I want to be magnificent.

I feel angry sometimes.

I feel really angry sometimes.

You were in charge Jake, you were always so sure of our path.

I am fed up with myself being a WWW (weepy, whiney, weenie), but putting on the big girl pants does not seem to be working

I really miss you guys. I am looking forward to being with

you again one day
I don't want to be fragile and broken.
I am strong....hahahaha right?
As the ultimate fixer, I can't believe I could not help you.
Soooooooooo, sorry.
I don't want to be dull. I want out of this dullness.
Where did I go?

And so, I would emote each morning when I stayed at Devora's newly named " Somis Serenity Ranch".

The pit in my stomach felt better as time progressed. Devora's magic was working.

I felt hopeful and stronger.

I was not a victim.

I would be emotionally available one day.

I would handle this change with grace and courage.....a rainbow warrior.

I got this....I got me.

My hardest time was still when I'd wake up and for a couple of split seconds, I'd think Jake was still alive, but then reality would set back in. I didn't feel safe without him in the world.

I knew he knew of everything and I was the wind beneath his wings.

Now, I had to be the wind under my own wings and learn how to fly solo.

I was so grateful for Devora and wanted to tread lightly around her home with respect.

I loved this farm, her sanctuary.

I came to realize that I would never stop loving Jake, but I couldn't feel badly enough to bring him back. I would have turned my insides out and poured acid all over myself to rid myself of this pain, sorrow and sadness.

I have never felt anything so disturbing in my whole life.

My love, you beat out Haley for that title.

I resisted at first, but Devora had a way of peeling my onion. She forced my stiff upper lip Brit to open up even when I just wanted to stuff it all back down inside myself.

She had two bedrooms upstairs but only a partial wall between them. Imagine a big attic vaulted ceiling farm space.

One evening, Devora was feeling down and so was I. We were talking to each other from our different beds – emoting, crying and feeling sad, sad, sad.

I think that may have been the straw that broke the camel's back. On returning the following week, the bed had been removed, and I was now to stay in the main house. I smiled. Of course, that made sense. Devora shared that both of us sobbing at the same time was just too much.

Devora would let me stay for a total of two nights and then send me home. I would sob and plead with her to let me stay, but she knew better than I, and indeed me going back to my Malibu train was the best next step for me. My little family would pack up and go back to my underwater domain where I would return to my life as a whale in excruciating pain, diving back into the water every time a huge grief wave came.

I would like to mention I have such gratitude and unending admiration for my beloved Devora, earth angel extraordinaire. She walked the talk and took us in. She calls me "Glenda the Good Witch" to this day.

What to do with myself?

I could not spend my life in bed.

This much I knew.

CHAPTER TWENTY-TWO

THE BEGINNING OF TRUE HEALING

By April the following year, I was still living in the Malibu train. Or maybe it was called existing. Friends and loved ones directed a lot of energy on me and insisted that I attend some kind of rehab for grieving.

"Why not?" I mused. Maybe it would help.

I was willing, but not sure which way to turn. A few weeks later, I booked a flight. I was still in a foggy haze and did my normal amount of research when it came to my stuff: zero. I glanced at the website for this facility and trusted my good friend who recommended the place. They read something about it. No one could quite remember, but they had heard of it.

So, I signed up.

I arrived at the Oakland airport, jumped on a shuttle and began what I hoped would be an amazing and transformational time of saying goodbye to Jake and Sam with dignity.

The Northern California facility was breathtaking because it was set high on a hill where hawks were known to soar. The house was beautiful with high ceilings and beautiful wood accents. I spotted a cozy living room, chalkboards and a lot of outside seating to enjoy the cool nights.

I was shown to a lovely bedroom located downstairs and was told that it would just be me in that room. I noticed that the facility was run by women and was told men weren't allowed.

"It's to give the women a safe place to share their feelings," I heard.

The first mission was to assemble in the living room where each of us in that small group of women was asked to hand over our cell phones. No outside contact was allowed. I remember feeling relief because I really didn't want to talk to anyone.

Nestling into a cushy, oversized chair, I waited to hear what the next two weeks would bring.

A beautiful, fair-haired woman who looked like a California surfer, introduced herself. She was in her early 30s and had the loveliest green eyes.

"Hello, I'm Katy," she said. "I just got released from a three-day hold at a psyche ward. I tried to kill myself. I am a prostitute."

My eyes began to widen.

Jade, in her 20s, jumped in. "Hello, I'm here because my ex got a restraining order against me. I have been to several rehabs and none worked," she said, adding with a smirk, "I think it's all bullshit."

She spoke with such clarity and strength for someone so young.

Brunette Claire, 40ish, was a pistol from New York. "I have been having an affair and I can't stop," she said.

It was my turn.

"Hello, I'm Deb," and with my new title for a country song I said. "I'm here to mourn my husband's suicide, my horse dying and losing my home."

OMG!

Where was I?

It didn't take long for all to become abundantly clear. I was at a love and sex addict's camp!

All of a sudden, my foggy brain began to wake up. No, this couldn't be possible. I hadn't had sex in years. I hadn't even been out for a cup of coffee with a man since Jake left. Where was my phone? I really needed to call Marie! We might never…ever…stop laughing.

Instead of dialing anyone, I slumped back in my chair knowing I had to make a quick decision. Should I stay or should I go? Look for the similarities, not the differences. And what the hell else are you doing for the next two weeks?

Gently, I exhaled and then returned to my bedroom where I burst into a fit of giggles. I mean, really?

A love and sex addicts' camp?

The next day, I attended a group session and participated. I was here and I wanted help. "Um, when do we get to the Jake/Sam mourning part?" I asked the other women. Everyone stared back at me with sympathetic, but puzzled eyes.

A little voice inside spoke to me. A penny in for a pound. Show up fully. You can learn something anywhere. And boy did I learn.

I was thrilled to hear that equine therapy was part of the program. It would be wonderful to see how these teachers conducted their sessions, so I went in with curiosity. I also loved the smell of the horses and the green, rolling hills. That day there were three other participants and we were led in a moving blessing where we raised our arms high into the sky. We gave thanks to the east, west, north and south.

I loved it!

Next, we were instructed to each hold onto a long rope and follow the leader into a field. Then we were asked to sit for ten minutes and just observe. On returning to the circle, we wrote what we had seen and shared it.

I went first. "I saw the most amazing baby lambs skipping over the horizon on green fields," I said. "I also saw beautiful baby birds flying high. I saw the most stunning majestic black horse sunbathing."

Katy went next. "I saw my big, black pimp with his huge dick hanging out."

It was a moment! How had I been trundling through life for all of these years thinking we understood each other? This was a massive life lesson that made me feel sorry for my kids.

Each individual will view life so differently. It's a miracle we're able to communicate with each other.

Our last task was to bless the horses for their service to us and then leave the energy clear for them. What a perfect way to end an enlightening and empowering day.

Back at the main rehab house, I noticed that a gentle bond was starting to form between all of us. It might have seemed odd to form this friendship since we came from different walks of life. My initial shyness was wearing off and I welcomed these new friends. At night, we would sit casually outside together and share our stories.

I learned that Jade was upset because she wasn't allowed to contact her boyfriend. The loss of her cell phone was sending her barreling into an anxiety attack.

That night while I rested in bed, I heard someone pacing the hallways. She pounded that hardwood floor at two a.m., three a.m., four a.m. and beyond. I was completely exhausted the next morning and still wasn't sure if those footsteps came from a human or a ghost.

It turned out that Jade had been in such an awful state that she was threatening to cut her wrists. All she wanted was that phone and the enforced withdrawal from her boyfriend wasn't going too well. I knew she was sleeping upstairs in a room on her own. It didn't take long for my inner Mom to come out in full force.

"Darling," I told her. "Would you maybe like it if I slept in the same room? I can move upstairs with you. No problem."

"Yes, please," said that beautiful girl.

Oh, to see this wonderful human torturing herself made me overflow with compassion.

At this sex and love clinic, I learned so much about living without judgment and coming from a place of pure love. The truth was I was falling in love with this place and the girls.

I heard about Katy's life and her history of working at different brothels. Her parents had tried to rescue her, and she was so mad at them. I just knew she had amazing rainbow goddess potential.

There came the day when I had the honor of sharing my story of how beyond life, we love our children. I explained that they don't come with instruction manuals. "As parents, we simply try to have the awareness we need in the moment," I said. Katy's parents had been put through the ringer since their precious daughter had tried to kill herself. I felt such love and empathy for them.

Another day, we were asked to make a tattoo/painting of what we had discovered about ourselves. I wrote: "I deserve to be heard."

I wondered why that came to mind.

I was told that I started this session apologizing for taking up too much room on the planet. I was too polite and not in touch with my authentic self. These were things I would work on in the future.

I did get to mourn Jake during this time and wrote him a letter.

My Darling Man:

You were the love of my life. I am so beyond sorry you are not here. I am so sorry we didn't find the answers to your sickness. I missed you so much as you faded from your lampshade over the past five years. Your light began to grow dimmer and dimmer. One day, you simply turned it off.

I know you have transcended back to source, but I don't know how to be on this planet without you. I have no idea of who I am, what I am supposed to do, or how to try and show up as the best version of myself. You kept me safe; you honored me; you protected me. I frickin' miss you.

How dare you leave me?

I am ripped wide open – naked, lonely and confused.

Darling, you always told me you would find me in every lifetime as your soulmate, beyond oceans of time. I can't wait for that day to come.

Now, I suffer. I wish I had an off button I could push because without you, I am utterly devoid of purpose. I can't say I wish I had loved you better because I did the best I could. Please know I was so blessed to call you my husband.

There is not a moment of each day that you are not with me.

Yet, the finality of death is miserable. I wish I could be whole again.

You were my man – intelligent, creative, Type A, a ball buster. You did not tolerate idiots. You were curmudgeonly, cranky, depressed, sad, lonely, tortured, disappointed and unwell.

I loved your whole being.

I know you know I would never have left you. I loved looking after you, my man.

I hate feeling sorry for myself. I have so much to be grateful for in life, but I miss you, my darling. I miss you.

I have to believe that you are alive in Nirvana, joyful and in peaceful bliss.

How do I put this experience to work for good? How do I keep on breathing?

One little foot in front of the other.

My man, I feel rootless. No one sees me as you did. I was so blessed and lucky. Your fairy on top of the Christmas tree. Your Glenda, the good witch. I have also lost my beloved Sampson. It would be his birthday tomorrow and your birthday on May 3.

I cannot be consoled.

Breathe, little Deb. Just keep breathing. One breath at a time.

I was able to read my letter to the other ladies and our mutual bond deepened with each layer of protection we discarded.

I was asked to write another life altering letter describing where I would like to see my life in one year.

So, I wrote:

Dear Deb:

You are light and joyful. You are no longer scared. You have roots, strong roots, and a community of amazing friends. You are adding to the planet and the joy of others. You are adding to the animals and giving them such joy. You come from compassion and passion.

You are healthy; not flailing around. You have another horse to love. You have your dogs. You will have a partner in the future who adores you.

You are gentle with yourself around the memory of Jake and Sampson.

Remember, you have a voice - a beautiful, pure, scorched in the fire voice. It says that you are of value. There is no one greater or less than you.

You will be more attuned at being gentle with other humans, at recognizing their pain body and stepping gently around it.

You will have -- "I don't need to be right, I need to be kind" -- ingrained in your memory.

You will safely be able to meet your authentic self and get in touch with your anger in a healthy way.

You will be gardening, interested and interesting; you will have continued learning about this journey, your dharma.

You will stand fully in your power as a magnificent rainbow goddess.

You will awake joyful, grateful, and singing a beautiful song about your life and your fellow humans each day.

When you have a negative thought, my darling Deb, you will be strong with the muscle of shift in your thought process.

You will then shine - shine, shine your inner light. That is your lightbulb.

You will be living in Santa Barbara; you will have found the perfect guesthouse.

You will have continued on your spiritual path.

You will have faith.

Darling Deb, you will have given yourself permission to move beyond the conventional life you have lived so far -- daughter, mother, wife and businesswoman.

Maybe in a year, you will be an explorer of the world, sail out from shore and not need a heavy anchor.

You will see this new chapter as a gift, continue to learn, and empower your little Debbie.

You are enough.

As time continued to unfold, I learned more and more each day including how to set boundaries around my well-being as a single person. What a concept – a good healthy concept.

There was a weekly Sunday trip to town and a local market day. The local car rally was fun although I was informed, we were not to wander and leave our chaperones. I guess love addicts have a way of scattering like cats never to be seen again. That left me chuckling.

Another great lesson was writing an invitation to your loved one. Mine read:

Darling Jake, my darling man:

You were the love of my life. I feel you with every breath, but I can't disappear into you. Here is how I'm going to hold you. When I meditate each morning, I shall gently send you white light from the ancient drusey stone of intention. When I close my eyes, I shall feel myself bathed in your love.

I have been so frozen, Jake. I'm in a state of shock, but I need to participate again in life, make some friends and laugh a little.

I loved knowing you for 27 years. I loved being your wife and a mother to your children. I loved you, but now I have to be here for me.

So, simple. So, complicated.

I can't wait for our energies to be intertwined again. It will be, but the blink of an eye. No greater love than one who sacrifices himself for another.

I shall always hold a sacred place for you, but I don't want to keep you here with my suffering. So, please enjoy heaven. Bathe in the starlight. Please don't stay bound to earth for me. I want you to be in bliss. No stress.

This is my invitation to you, my darling man.

Before I left this magical place, we had a burning ceremony to celebrate our journeys through life. It was so powerful and cleansing.

As I packed to go home, I knew I'd miss my new tribe because I loved each of them. At our final closing ceremony, we were each given an angel bracelet and each participant infused the angel with a word that reminded them of each other.

As I was leaving, one of the owners took me to the side.

"Perhaps we'll meet again," she said. "You never know, Deb. You could be a love addict one day.

I smiled, "Well, I guess you never know."

CHAPTER TWENTY-THREE

VISIONS OF THE FUTURE

After love addict's camp, I started to make a vision board for my new life. It was important cutting and pasting things from magazines, a daily reminder of what I would like to attract into my life. This is such a powerful tool and I'd suggest that anyone give it a try no matter what you're trying to draw into your life.

I got the word "faith" tattooed onto my wrist, a beautiful instant reminder whenever I needed it.

God sent a really loud message that it was time to move. The twelve and thirteen-year-old kidlets that lived above the train were lovely but were often left with a nanny while their parents worked. The older daughter liked to jump off the bed right onto my head for hours on end. It was utterly unrelenting, and my dogs and I quivered together at night in bed as we heard, "Thud, thud, thud." It felt like we were in a war zone and my PTSD kicked in.

Still wobbly with my coping skills, I called upstairs and left a couple of messages. The ceilings were low in the train, so the jumping was literally inches above my frazzled face. At the same time, I spoke with Devora and Marie who both felt that Malibu wasn't a healthy location for me because there were too many memories there with Jake.

Bumping into a neighbor at the post office who had not heard of Jake's transition, I was trying to recite my "bad country song" as quickly as possible without hurting the human hearing the news for the first time. It hurt to drive past my kidlets' old schools or my old home. The list went on and on.

On Craig's List, I saw a picture of a guesthouse with a big iron horse in the garden, located in Santa Barbara.

A sign?

Immediately, I called the landlord to set an appointment to see the rental on that Monday only to receive a call on Sunday saying it had been taken.

Ok, not a sign.

Over the prior year, I had a single friend named Bertha who lived in Santa Barbara. She invited my dog Jack and I to stay for a couple of weekends that were quite blissful.

"Deb, we could be just like sisters. It will be wonderful," she said.

I told Marie who asked, "How well do you know her?"

"Well, she can be a little prickly," I said. "But I think I will cheer her up."

Sadly, I gave notice in Malibu to begin a new chapter that would

242

mark my sixth move in two and a half years. It turns out that moving in with Bertha was the wrong choice. She had questions: "Why are your nails such a bright color? Why is your hair so blonde? Why is your furniture so ugly and large? Why on earth did you bring bricks?"

The straw that broke the camel's back was sitting on the floor in my bedroom at her house and crying huge, heart wracking sobs. I called Devora and said, "I'm in crisis." I couldn't move back to the Malibu train as it already had been rented out, but even with the thumping, it was better than this spiteful energy coming at me in unexpected waves.

Devora scooped me up for dinner and we met a wonderful, new earth angel named Anne-Marie. It was decided that my furniture would stay with Bertha whom I gave the needed six weeks' notice. I'd go back to sofa surfing. Jackie kindly let me sleep at her home and I also stayed with Devora, but I once again felt rootless, floating off of the planet, scared and unsure. The feeling of fear wouldn't leave me. I kept repeating to myself that fear was false evidence appearing real. But it seemed pretty real to me. I kept wondering what the hell I was doing.

Jack and I were displaced once again.

All I thought I had wanted was to live with another human being, as long as they were breathing.

I guess I needed another criteria, as the energy someone emits is as important as the breathing part.

I continued to look on Craig's List until one day I saw the iron horse again. How could that be possible? I held my breath and called. Yes, there was someone else living in the home, but she had given notice as she did not like the teenagers living in the main house. I said, "Well, as long as they're not jumping on beds that connect with the ceiling of my bedroom, I love teenagers."

I moved into my Santa Barbara hug, as I called it. It's a detached guesthouse on two acres of land. My landlord has turned out to be one of the kindest humans on the planet and I adore his children.

Even so, the first couple of days in my new hug home were overwhelming. Once again, I found myself with way too much furniture because this space was much smaller than the Malibu train. I wept tears for myself as I shed more of my past.

Then I remembered to flex my shift button. Another small storage unit was rented. Things were given away. Suddenly, my hug looked like a home.

Now, it was time to shine. I repeated: "My peace and serenity are precious to me. They live in this hug."

I truly believe that "when God closes a door, He opens a window. But it's hell in the hallway."

My lesson was that I didn't want to live with an unhappy human. I would much rather be filled with joy as I walked through my own front door.

This was huge progress towards independence.

CHAPTER
TWENTY-FOUR

THERAPY ROCKS

One day Jackie collected me and literally walked me into the hospice to make an appointment. I would meet my therapist Marilyn. What a Godsend.

At first, it felt awkward; I would say a sentence and then want to know how she was feeling about it. I am happy to say after a year of those sessions; I plop down on the couch now and really dig deep. I must unload and look at my behavior in order to grow.

Marilyn took time counseling me about the importance of gently re-growing my roots again. "Deb, you don't need to buckle under pressure to go and visit people and stay with them. Just ground yourself here," she advised.

OMG. ….. the relief those words provided.

My hug of a house seemed so important now. Equally brilliant was when Marilyn told me, "Deb, you are allowed to change your mind. You can say yes, no, yes and no again."

I had always been a responsible person of my word, so this was an absolute revelation to me. The feeling of being crazy seemed to evaporate. The truth was I no longer had to operate my life from duty, but now I had permission to check in with my authentic self. I loved my daughter, my stedaughter and stepson, but they had to live their own lives. I could say yes…and no. Even to them.

Around this time, my friend Ava also encouraged me to keep looking for a horse because that's what gave me ultimate joy. I did an Internet search each day until I found my joy. He is a gentle, magnificent wonder named Patron.

I wondered if I could change his name to Julio.

My friends laughed. "His name is perfect. Go and visit Argentina if you want to find a Julio," they teased me.

My world expanded exponentially with my new friend Patron who I moved to a very rustic barn with a lot of amazing horsewoman trail riders. These wonderful humans began to enter my life as if they were just waiting for the right moment to appear.

Patron quickly became the center of my world and my new love.

Somewhere over those months, I had another not-so-bright idea to move Patron to the Four Seasons of barns. I felt a different vibe there and it wasn't as relaxed as my beloved rustic barn. The old Deb might have just done a work-around. The new Deb, with some counseling from Marilyn, gave notice to the Four Seasons barn and begged my first barn to let us back. When they did, I had a much deeper appreciation of being there. I embraced the dirt and dust.

It was a learning curve I wouldn't soon forget.

I wasn't spending all my time on horseback either. Ava encouraged me to sign up for a mediation certification course in Santa Monica. The course was a weeklong and at the end, I would be able to join

Mediators without Boarders and travel anywhere in the world where they needed a peacekeeping mediation.

I learned so much, but ultimately decided it was not my calling as I really don't like people arguing. I have the urge to say, "Really? That's what you have your knickers in a twist about?"

My new business cards made me laugh.

Deb Richards
Holy Fire Reiki Master
Angel Card Reader
Dog Walker
Equine Therapist
Mediator Without Boarders

Little did I know that all of these skills would help in my own spiritual growth, which is truly a never-ending quest along paths beautifully unknown.

I'll never forget one occurrence I had before I left Malibu. Another friend who is a medium told me, "Deb, Jake doesn't like being under your bed. He wants a different space." With that new knowledge, I moved his ashes into the storage unit with Pluto, my beloved puppy who had also transcended.

Time passed and eventually, I told Ava that I needed to find Jake's ashes again. "I don't know where they are in the storage locker," I said. "It's so full of stuff. But I want to ship his ashes to the kidlets."

My judge friend Ava was up for the task. On a pitch-black evening, she went with me to the dreaded storage unit where we were armed with two flashlights. We had baseball caps on that made it feel like a Special Ops mission.

Into the creepy space we went.

"Do you know it's illegal to ship ashes over state lines?" Ava told me.

Me: "Ava, take off your fricking judge's hat and just be my friend tonight. Its Thelma and Louise time."

We dug through the stuff that was tightly packed from floor to ceiling. I had to move past Jake's clothes, family pictures and that huge dining room table that was the setting of so many happy family memories. There was so much stuff. It was the remains of my former life.

I started to panic and wondered if we would ever find him. What kind of mother was I? Did I lose their father's ashes? I felt so defeated and alarmed as we climbed through each pile.

"Deb, maybe Jake likes it in here," Ava said. "Maybe he wants to be with all of his stuff."

I took a breath because perhaps she was right. But just as we were about to pull the rolling door back down – mission aborted – out of the corner of my eye, I saw a box that was labeled PLUTO. "OMG, Ava, Jake's in there. I put him with Pluto so he would not be so lonely."

Both of us believed that divine intervention led us to Jake's ashes at the last possible moment.

In the end, Jake and Pluto's ashes came home to my beloved hug with me. Eventually, I would have a scattering of Jake, Sampson, Pluto and any other ashes I possessed. Their new home would be the gorgeous Santa Barbara ocean. It seemed so fitting because I look at the ocean each day and I shall know that the ashes have been repurposed.

Ashes to ashes. Dust to dust.

During my therapy sessions, Marilyn validated my feelings about life,

"You are allowed to mourn all you have lost, but don't be so harsh judging yourself," she advised. "Would you speak to a friend in the way you speak to yourself?"

Of course, the answer was always "no." I would never speak to another human in the way my exacting self-talk was delivered to me, myself and I.

I had an in-depth conversation with Marilyn about Jake's passing and how to talk about it. I told her that people always wanted to know how Jake had transitioned, I would always promptly reply "heart attack."

Was I lying?

With her normal practicality and wisdom, she told me that what I was doing was absolutely fine. I was in fact protecting myself from other humans. If the reaction were unkind, the energy would have engulfed me and reopened the fragile eggshell I had developed. Once again, I would be shattered.

Every morning I would meditate and light a memorial candle for Jake. I was better, but with each breath I drew in, I was still fighting for my survival. I would chat to myself, "Shift Deb, shift that painful thought, you can shift it. Ok, now shine, go get dressed, walk your talk, save yourself and shine."

Marilyn taught me about grief waves where you must catch your breath, breathe and dive under the wave. You can allow yourself to cry, knowing that you will come out on the other side. "Soon Deb, you will hear my voice in your head even when I'm not with you," Marilyn promised.

I couldn't wait.

I even made a diagram for Marilyn and divided it up into a pie chart. There were several slices, in no particular order, and they included:

- Alanon/Therapy
- Horse riding/Continue improving my skills
- Spiritual learning/Attend meetings at Verdanta temple, Lake Shrine and Agape center.
- Work out/Pilates
- Work/Be of service
- Treasure my friends, my earth angels/ Tell them always how much I love them at every chance I get.
- FUN/ Dance (like no one is watching…hahaha I have that one down)
- Get Happy/ Dance to the happy song whenever I hear it, whatever I am doing.
- And finally…..
- Love, love and love some more/Unconditional love.

Marilyn was really pleased with my progress.

"Deb, you are healing," she said.

Yes, yes, yes, I was.

I had not been able to say the word suicide when I first started seeing Marilyn. I preferred to say, "Transitioned by choice." There is so much stigma attached to suicide, but I was dealing with it, surviving and gradually thriving.

These days, I can feel the joy slowing creeping back into my heart. Now, I smile back at the slightly younger me with love. Marilyn has taught me that you can feel overwhelming pain and absolutely uplifting joy within seconds of each other. She has given me permission to get in touch with how I feel.

I say yes.

I say no.

It's my choice.

I'm also learning to parent myself, so the wild teenager that still lurks within me doesn't take over. I've also soothed the frightened child with each gentle breath and sweet smile. When I notice myself going into a panic attack mode about how the next ten years will unfold and how I will tick all the correct boxes, I gently remind myself that we shall all transition. We don't get to take any of our "stuff" with us. The most important thing is for me to show up each day as the best me, a little better than the me of yesterday.

I need to enjoy all the other humans with their lampshades and beautiful inner light bulbs burning brightly.

I've started to say, "Yes, why not?" It has replaced, "No, I can't."

At this age, I understand what it means to be spontaneous.

Case in point: One of the ways I recently filled my happiness bucket to overflowing was accepting an invitation to crew on a 61-foot yacht called Taxi Dancer. The captain smiled when I asked if this boat could tip over.

"Nope, she has been around the world."

I felt some relief and a little safer.

Oh, it wasn't a breezy little cruise.

My spot that night was mainly on my knees, crawling from one side of the boat to the other to avoid the boom beheading me. There was that moment when I honestly felt we'd tip over sideways. During a lot of frantic yelling of directions when things looked dicey, I heard, "Rail meat, move! Move NOW!"

At one point, I had to dangle my arms and legs over the side as the ocean waves swept up and soaked me with spray. Oh, the surge of adrenaline that pumped through my system. Oh, the absolute joy! I felt so connected to source and so joyfully at one with my man, Jake, and my horse, Sampson. My eyes filled with tears as I felt their love staying with me. I felt like shouting up to the heavens, "Hey guys, look at me! I feel you! I feel you! I shall always feel you! It's your little Deb having an adventure."

They knew.

BIRTHDAYS, CHRISTMAS AND A NEW YEAR

My birthday on October 30 was fast approaching and this marked my second without Jake and Sam. I wondered what I might do. Devora and Marie asked me to go dancing with them. OMG! I love to dance although I probably only know one dance. I still make it work to any music.

I asked if we could actually go to an old western saloon across the mountains in the Santa Ynez Valley, and try our hand at country dancing.

I got a quick yes. We could do whatever I wished.

My 73-years-young landlord had asked me stop by his coffee shop that morning to meet all of his friends who had been gathering in the same spot for 35 years. It's a group of men only. Needless to say, it felt special. I love my landlord because he is one of the coolest humans ever.

After, I met Jackie for a champagne brunch and the time was filled with such love and gratitude shining through me. Then I was off for a hair appointment where I joined Marie and Devora. We had lunch at the Boat House, set up by a friend name Darci. We ate outside, right on the ocean, all ten of us. I felt so sparkly and so loved by these amazing women in my life.

The next stop was a drive over the mountain into the beautiful wine district of Santa Ynez for dinner, which included even more friends.

I felt as if I had just turned 21 when I made a mad dash to the hotel to change into my party dress and cowboy boots. Mavericks, here we come! When we walked into the country bar, the place was empty, but my girlfriends are such great sports that they didn't care. We went out on that empty dance floor and moved around to the live band like we were at our first prom. Whoooo hoooo! I was having so much fun.

Soon, the empty saloon began to fill with people and I felt good, happy and most of all, alive.

Out of nowhere, a handsome younger man by about two decades made it his mission to twirl me around to every song while I felt pure exhilaration. My inner teenager was out on the town!

At one point, I glanced across a now crowded dance floor to see my friend Monica, who is insanely beautiful, dancing with a guy who was pushing 80. He had no teeth. We laughed so much that night, connected with each other and felt the joy of having magic around us. It was a magic that we made.

I was showing up for life again.

In that moment, I knew that life could be so very joyful.

Marie said the best part was breakfast the next morning when we all appeared in shades. Fragile would be the word to describe our condition, but we all cracked up reliving the night before.

253

Thanksgiving rolled around and it was just my beloved dog and I. Frankly, I didn't feel like hanging out with anyone else's family although I was grateful for the options.

In the end, it was just a frozen microwave turkey dinner, a warm bed, and my dog Jack snuggling with me, which was absolutely perfect. It was also a great lesson. It wasn't the end of the world to spend the day this way. It was just a Thursday in my life.

Christmas was soon approaching, and Marilyn and I made another plan. We were going to have me do the un-Christmas version of the holiday, which meant no presents. It would just be another day. It was just a Friday.

Shift and shine, my friends.

I could have dwelled on it being a lonely Christmas, but I refused and shifted my thoughts when they went to dark places. Think of your mind like a muscle that you move. I'm getting better at this each and every day.

The point is to shine my light source , shine my lightbulb and then shift and shine again and again.

So, what became of that Christmas? My friend Monica was here staying with friends and we had arranged to see each other Christmas afternoon. She was also going through some life-altering experiences and wanted quiet time to write a letter. She called me at 2:30 p.m. and said, "I need a wine break. Shall I come and get you?" Monica is so filled with life and has a smile so huge, it's absolutely infectious.

It turns out all the resorts in Santa Barbara were open on Christmas. Monica had a plan. "Let's do our own trifecta of resorts."

"Yes," I replied. "Sounds like fun."

Oh my God, it was fun with fun sprinkled on top. As we walked into the lobby of the Four Seasons Biltmore, my mouth dropped open. We had stumbled upon a Christmas Disney movie. Every employee was in a Santa hat and the tree was exquisitely twinkling and decorated so fabulously in gold and silver. My eyes couldn't take in enough of this splendor.

A table miraculously opened for us in a spot where we could see the ocean. We invited a chap who was on his own to join us and proceeded to order appetizers. Everyone was in such a good mood. When Monica and I asked Chap Number One (and yes, there would be more) to take our picture, Chap Number Two photo bombed us. Laughter was everywhere.

I was still in my riding clothes from earlier that day, which made it the perfect, low-key Christmas. But we weren't done. The second stop was the El Encanto with sweeping, majestic views of the Pacific Ocean. If you sit there for five minutes, you're mentally in the South of France.

By now, a brisk winter wind danced across the ocean and we sat there bravely being blown away. "Monica, do you think it's a tad chilly, darling?" I inquired. She burst out laughing as we were about to be sucked off our chairs into a tornado of wind.

We wouldn't quit, but moved under a wonderful heat lamp and split fish and chips. Fabulous!

Our next stop was the San Ysidro Ranch and the walkway twinkled with fairy lights that had been placed in all the old olive trees. From there, we moved to the Plow and Angel Pub, which was like walking into that old TV series, *Cheers*. The pub had a burning fireplace, soft lighting and massive holiday decorations.

Monica and I marveled at how well this was working out. We

were having a magical Christmas without having to do any of the decorating or clean up! Everyone was so friendly that I wished the holiday spirit could extend for the other 364 days of the year. Talk about a global shift and shine!

We ended our day back at the Four Seasons Biltmore where we knew the staff and enjoyed a feeling of camaraderie. As we walked around, we heard a band playing in their stunning ballroom. Could life get any better? I looked at Monica; she looked at me. We proceeded to dance our feet off. One chap even approached us afterwards and said, "Your performance, you girls dancing, well it just made my evening."

Yes, we were spreading sunshine on a dark Christmas night.

Monica spent the night at my hug house. In bed, we laughed and recounted the day and all the wonderful people we met in these gorgeous fairylands. Our un-Christmas, it was decided, would become a new tradition.

Whoosh! It was New Year's Eve and my girlfriends had dragged me out with them to a champagne bar and celebration. I wasn't sure…but they were. I was going.

An extremely handsome French man asked me to dance. This man was attentive and fun. I felt pretty for the first time in forever.

He danced every dance with me, and I made it until midnight, which may not sound like a big deal, but was in stark contrast to the prior year, where I was in bed by 7 p.m., alone, lonely and not wanting to participate with other humans in festivities at all.

I smiled at this man, another positive change and a whisper of a possibility.

We spent time together over the next months, and my landlord

Bob bumped into the French guy bringing me coffee early one morning. It was awkward for both of them because no male had been near my hug home in all the months I had lived there.

When I saw Bob the next day, my conversation went like this:

"It's true Bob," I told him with a smile and twinkle. "I've taken a younger French lover"

"Good for you honey!" he said, "Good for you."

Life continued on. The lovely French man faded from my life after several months, and in time, I did meet someone else. The someone else was hugely popular, and we used to laugh that he had to ask me out as he had dated everyone else in our hometown!

I told Marie about him, and she wisely counselled me to have the following conversation;

So when I next saw him, I turned beet red and blurted out, "Have you had a recent STD test?"

His bright, green eyes sparkled back at me. "Well, that's such a strange question to start the evening off with," he replied.

My dating skills were lacking. I felt as if I was 16 again, and not in a good way as I dubbed myself clumsy and inadequate. I had zero skills.

It occurred to me "Dating for Dummies" could be my next book!

HEAVEN CAN WAIT

A year prior, I had stopped seeing my amazing therapist, Marilyn. There was a waiting list for her to see others and I figured that I was over the worst part of my grieving and other humans needed to see her. But as I was approaching the third anniversary of Jake's transition, I suddenly felt wobbly again.

Then for a week, I forgot my morning ritual to shift and shine, (crash and burn would be more appropriate) I had been out at a group event, but still felt waves of loneliness and grief. I came home distraught. I felt isolated. I lay on the bed sobbing, thinking about Jack, my beloved Jack Russell who had transitioned ten months earlier. My little hug felt so empty with no four-legged friend to keep me company. I had resisted getting another dog as I didn't want to go through that pain of loss again.

Despite my best efforts I missed them, I missed my life, I missed him.

I simply missed him.

I thought about my children, grown with families now of their own. They were all in really good places at that time.

My friends were also happy and content. I also had made arrangements for my horse, Patron to go to Marie if anything ever happened to me.

As I lay there, my body convulsing and crying to the heavens, I had a moment of clarity.

I, too, would transcend by choice. I would go to Jake, Sampson and Jack. I wanted to be held in his arms once more and run my fingers through his thick hair and kiss those lips. I would slip my hand into his one more time. I would be at peace; we would all be reunited. My light had dimmed over the past week; my life's energy finally depleted.

I had been on sleeping pills since Haley's relapse and the night terrors had made sleeping impossible. I stopped taking the pills and was rather proud of myself. It also meant that I had two months of pills – or 60 of them.

So, I sat on my bed with the pills and a nice rosé wine to wash them down. I stuffed them into my mouth, heaving, gagging, swallowing. This took all of ten minutes. I climbed under the covers and waited to go to sleep. I couldn't wait to be reunited.

Then my phone rang. It was a girlfriend Lisa calling me from New York. I was crying into the phone, my conversation unintelligible. She called Jackie and said, "You need to go over and see Deb. She sounds awful."

Jackie tried calling me, but I had switched my phone off. Frantic, she decided to drive by my hug and found me unconscious.

She called 911....I don't remember the ambulance ride or my stomach being pumped. The experience for Jackie was horrible, and I regret that deeply.

However, I died.

They brought me back.

"Wow, this is not heaven"

That was my first thought when I opened my eyes. When I focused, I saw

Eileen, Anne, Marie, Kat and Devora at the end of my bed. All of the faces I loved.

Marie smiled and gently said, "Deb, what did you think…that Jake, Sampson and Jack would be there in a room waiting for you?

Marie followed up with, "For God's sake, take your lashes off," she said. "You look like a movie star laying there"

Eileen would tell me later that I took enough pills to take out an elephant. My biggest sadness was Jackie going through all the trauma of finding me.

I spent three days in the psychiatric ward where I gradually lifted my head out of my overwhelming depression and anxiety. Was it selfish? Yes, but my need for Jake was greater.

Natasha commented "Debmama, do you want to make my parents' lives into a Shakespearian tragedy? My Dad transcended and Debmama did too!"

I came home to my hug and moved all my furniture around; the place is only 700 square feet. Rearranging wasn't an easy task, but I wanted it to feel different.

I started meditating, praying and turning my will over to God.

Once again, I began asking, "How may I serve? How may I serve….coming from gratitude?"

Kat commented in her frank wonderful way, "Well Deb, you obviously have more work to do down here. Heaven can wait."

So, after working on this memoir for twelve years, I decided maybe it was time to put a period. Finish it. Maybe it's part of my purpose.

I had known Jake since I was 27.

I am now heading toward my 60th birthday.

Our story was one that needed to be told in case it could be of service to one…or many.

Anne and I went to the pound as soon as I was released. I fell instantly in love with a huge husky named Tundra. I asked Bob if I might adopt such a big dog

His reply made me happy. "Sure, honey"

With much excitement, I brought this dog home. He slept on the bed next to me this first night and took up half of the bed! My bed finally felt full up in a way it had not before.

I decided to take Tundra to the local pet store because he needed more toys.

Inside the store, he growled, spun and lurched at a cute little dog. He even went for his throat, OMG!!

The little dog's owner was pissed off and rightfully so. I explained in a shaky voice that I had just rescued him from the pound.

"Well," he said dryly, "Now you know something more about him"

Once again, huge sobs, tears rolling down my face, I knew what I had to do.

At the pound, they were wonderful. "Please don't cry, Tundra will be fine. Now, we have more information about him"

I was devastated.

I met Anne for lunch the following day at our local western bar and grill that had comforting low lights for my swollen eyes. "I think I need another dog; maybe a Westie. My Mom and stepfather had one," I told her.

We began looking online and all the prices were insane. Then a little white face popped up. Six hundred dollars. Delivered all the way from Alabama. I took a big breath, pushed purchase and could not wait for her to arrive.

I decided to name her Daisy Mae as an homage to those Southern roots.

At the airport, she was shaken and covered in flees, so off to the vet we went. Much to his delight, the doc found a strain of worm that can only be contracted in that part of America. Everything was fixable.

I've had Daisy Mae for about two years now and she sleeps on my bed and covers my eyes, nose and mouth with kisses each morning. I tell Daisy as we are mouth to mouth, I hope she has not recently killed a goffer! My hug is alive again. My heart is full again with this little runt of the litter. She's happiness on four legs and I adore her. The funny thing is she looks exactly like a female version of Jack!

In the past year, I have been able to be of service, helping people who have lost loved ones, transition by choice, but also any kind of transition. I have been a sounding board for family members who are in the middle of addiction.

Yes, I am insanely grateful to be here.

Yes, life is worthwhile every day.

Yes, my light bulb is burning brightly.

EPILOGUE

One last word about love, at least on these pages. I find myself in the fourth year after my husband transcended still living in Santa Barbara in my hug house. I no longer have dreams where I wake up thinking Jake is still alive. I have the quiet acceptance that can only come with time.

Since I started writing this book twelve years ago, so many things have changed and so many have stayed the same.

I am still single, I have become accustomed to living on my own, and if there is never to be another love like Jake for me, that's ok. My complicated, amazing intelligent man, I realize how blessed I was to have had that love once in my life, where he made me feel like the fairy on top of the Christmas tree.

I am blessed to have many many earth angels, and if I shift and shine every day, Jake is smiling at me and I feel his love.

Natasha grew up into the most amazing, kind, thoughtful, responsible human. She had a baby boy, and gave him Jake as his middle name. He will turn three soon and sparkles just like his Mom.

Her husband is the same young man from 12 years ago when she was 15.

I would find out as time passed, that I was wrong in blaming him for leading my angel astray. It was in fact Natasha, saying, "Try this... swallow that."

He has qualified as a Fire Fighter and I could not be prouder and happier for their future.

I can talk with her about anything and everything. She brings me great comfort.

This past Mother's Day, she wrote to me: "You taught me that to be kind is way more important than being right, to love with my whole heart, and to never miss the beauty in nature".

My stepson is happy, healthy and has his own young family and a wonderful wife. I remember with fondness when I was once complaining about the girls, he said to me, "Well, Deb, if this was a baseball game, one out of three would be really good." God bless him.

Haley's father was killed in a tragic car accident in France when he was rear ended into a tree. I found myself feeling so badly that I sat down and meditated. Through the power of prayer, I told him I forgave him.

I wish I could tie a neat bow around this story for you, however I continue to struggle with Haley. She has taught me to focus on shining my light even when things are far from perfect. She is sober, halleluiah! However, she is a dry drunk, refusing to get the help from

Alcoholics Anonymous that would help her so much.

I find the meth affected her skills in so many ways. Her mental age has been stunted and that mixed with the severe ADHD has made it a struggle for me to decide when I am enabling and when I am helping.

Haley has years where it seems calm, and I am beyond grateful for those reprieves, followed by years of absolute chaos and turmoil.

Recently, she was living in her car in the Burger King parking lot with her new boyfriend her and dog. I refused to help. A friend mentioned how hard it is to get on your feet if you are homeless. Of course, I felt so badly that both of her fathers had died, and I was the only one to make the decision. I wished I had someone to hold my hand and tell me it's all going to be OK.

Eventually, I decided to help them get into a rental far away from me, which serves as another layer of self-protection. She is on occasion delusional, but I hold myself steady. She is clean.

I tell myself, "Detach with kindness. Respond and don't react. Where there is hope, maybe there is always a way."

I practice what has saved my life.

Shift your thought…shine your light.

Something else about Jake: I sat down the other day to be a grown up and do paperwork when a song he wrote that you know, that everyone knows – "I Love Rock and Roll" – started blasting out of the radio. I sat with that and asked myself how I felt. I listened all the way through until the next song began to play. The title? "Because I'm Happy." Then I heard, "God Only Knows," which is a song Jake played for me all the time.

I knew Jake was talking to me and I still miss him every single day, but in a gentle way. He comes to me in dreams where we're reunited in a special place. Sometimes, I write the dreams down; sometimes I just let them wash away.

As I feel safe with new earth angel friends, I have been able to share how Jake transcended from the planet. I have only been greeted with compassion and kindness. In fact, my friend Kat, newly widowed, had such an interesting conversation with me. She said, "It's not how someone died, but how they lived."

We're all transcending. What we do today in the now is absolutely what counts. Do we smile and share kind words? Do we add to the collective joy and hope for humanity?

My dream for the future is to open Shift and Shine: The Healing Ranch and serve humans and horses that need help.

My time is also spent learning how to sail as I've discovered I have an absolute passion for being out on the ocean. It soothes my soul. My goal was to have my sailing certificate by the second anniversary of Jake transcending. I'm sooo happy to say that I succeeded. I gathered my earth angels that morning for the memorial sail and to scatter Jake and Sampson's ashes.

I saw Devora approaching me and she was engulfed in huge sobs.

"Not today," I said, hugging her, "Today is about joy."

In the end, the captain took us out on a much bigger boat that I'm not qualified to sail. However, once clear of the harbor, he gamely turned the wheel over to me and took off for the other end of the boat. Jackie, Devora and Marie were suddenly screaming because we were heading into the rocks on the sea wall. I screamed for the captain to come and help me.

Apparently, the steering was opposite from how I had learned.

The girls teased me about my *I Love Lucy* moment. Meanwhile, Marie, who grew up sailing, was poised and ready to take the wheel from me at any moment.

We anchored out at sea and then scattered beautiful roses. Jackie read a prayer and I scattered the ashes of Jake and Sampson. As the boat gently swayed, we shared stories of both and I cried, laughed… and then laughed and cried some more.

Oh my God! What an amazing, deep, and at times painful journey.

I call it my life.

AFTERWORD

My favorite chant is:

Om mani padme hum

The jewel in the lotus.

The lotus appears pure, white and unblemished out of the muddy waters

The lotus had to push through the mud to appear in the light of day.

Embrace the struggle to attain the enlightenment.

Let's all shift and shine. My heart pours into yours, whoever you may be with light and love.

Deb

XOXO

APPENDIX

Here are the sayings I have taped to my computer. They're bite size reminders to me every single day. I hope that in darkness and light, they resonate with you. Feel free, dear readers, to add to my list!

This is what gets me through the days:

*True nobility is being better than I used to be.
*Let go. Let God decide.
*You did not cause it. You can't control it. You can't cure it.
*Most of the shadows of this life are caused by standing in one's own sunshine.
*Is this the hill I want to die on?
*Love in action.

*DDD - Deb the Demon Destroyer.

*Detach. Don't abandon.

*Put a bottom in your happiness bucket, and water daily.

*IL Belle Far Niente. (The beauty of doing nothing) (thank you John)

*Row your own boat gently down the stream.

*Nobody else's.

*They have their own oars…really.

People have asked me about the mediation I do each day for people with A.D.D.

I light an incense stick.

I pop on my headset, and listen to *Gamma Meditation System 2.0* by Dr Jeffrey Thompson

It is the most soothing music, and helps to put you into a meditative state.

I sit on a pillow.

I raise my arms to heaven and say, "Good morning, Father Rah. Good morning Mother Earth."

I then call on white, gold and silver light to enter my body through my crown chakra, infusing my body with love to every single cell within me, health, humility, courage, moderation, intelligence and empathy.

I then read a page from the following books,

Forgiving and Moving On by Tian Dayton, PH.D.

Daily Guidance from my Angels by Doreen Virtue

Change your Thoughts, Change Your Life, Living the Wisdom of the Tao by Dr. Wayne Dyer

The Soul of Healing Affirmations by Depak Chopra and Donna D'Cruz

Messages from the Universe, Mike Dooley

I then set my egg timer for seven minutes.

I close my eyes and say, "Ommmsaaaa."

I try to gently bring my energy to my third eye in-between my eyebrows.

When the egg timer rings, I place my hands on my drusy stone with the power of intention.

I again close my eyes.

I then, speaking out loud, say:

"Please send blessings to my children and my children's children. May they leave the planet better than they found it. May they be surrounded by earth and sky. Angels always."

"Please bring blessings for all my earth angel friends, I love them all soooooo much. Please may I bring blessings to them."

"Hi Jake, my man, I love you, I hope you are proud of me, I hope you are smiling and rocking heaven baby."

"Love to all my blessed creatures."

"Love to the universal love bank, for all humans everywhere."

"Please Universe send courage that the words might come from you onto the paper, that they might help one human in pain."

And in closing, I put my hands together in prayer and say,

"Thank you, thank you, thank you.

How may I serve? How may I serve? How may I serve?"

This starts my day off beautifully, and keeps my feet firmly planted on our beautiful planet.

ACKNOWLEDGEMENTS

There have been so many amazingly kind and compassionate earth angels in my life that have helped me to put one foot in front of the other.

Thanks so my joyful sister Tish, in the UK.

Cindy Pearlman my editor my gently encouraging me when I finally delivered the book four years after I was supposed to.

John Stenzel for being a true hero, selfless and kind.

Marie, I really don't have words for my unending gratitude, but for always standing shoulder to shoulder with me and holding my hand, and never abandoning me.

Kenny for introducing me to my husband, Jake.

Exey for her kindness to me, courage and always lending a helping hand.

Devora for nudging me every day to keep writing and believing in the healing power of the story. For holding my hand, even at 3am.

Ava for making sure I did not drown in a grief wave.

Rachel for her help with all the animals.

Jackie for being my rock and literally my life saver.

Lisa, who called me on that fateful night and makes me smile.

Claire and Chris who jumped right in to help.

Lawrence and Alice.

James, my stepson, for being such an absolute love through all of this.

Marcella and Steve for always having a spare bed for me.

Monica for being a breath of fresh air, and truly the wind beneath my wings.

Bob, my beloved landlord.

Anne who teaches me courage under pressure.

Kat, with whom I am forever grateful for helping me on this journey.

Sheila for her encouragement to never give up.

Juli and Rochelle for their kindness and for always including me.

One final shout out to Monica and Jackie for the final push, in finding my spelling mistakes, etc, and giving me a deadline! It really did take a village!!

And of course, my daughters, Haley and Natasha who without their blessing this book would not see the light of day.

Many other earth angels who touch my life daily, thank you.

And my greatest teacher, Dr Wayne Dyer.

ABOUT THE AUTHOR

Deborah lives in her beloved Santa Barbara with her Westie, Daisy, and Patron, her horse. She continues to be a life coach and equestrian therapist.

Deborah can be reached at Deborahshines@gmail.com

John Stenzel can be reached at jcarlstenzel@gmail.com

www.deborahshines.com

Lastly for people with addicts in their lives: the most important thing, do not be an ostrich like I was. Denial wastes so much precious time.

Always choose a same sex rehabilitation hospital.

Always lend a hand for recovery.

If you are not sure, get a drug test performed.

Read everything you can so that you learn quickly what you don't know, you don't know.

Detach but don't abandon.

Respond, don't react.

Please be gentle with yourself

Codependent No More, by Melody Beattie.

For humans who have lost someone to transition by choice, Abraham Hicks have an amazing CD on this subject.

The Afterlife of Billy Fingers by Annie Kagan, has helped me soooo much, I keep copies to hand out when other humans are in pain. This book is a wonderful read for anyone who has lost someone.

Anything by Dr Wayne Dyer.

Many Lives, Many Masters written by Dr Brian L Weiss

I personally have come to believe we all visit this planet many times, we agree to the big things that happen in our lives, saying, "Yes, I can do that"

For the lessons learnt, the compassion and empathy it will bring us.

We pick our parents, our loved ones, time and time again in different roles.

With each visit, we move a little higher in our vibration level.

Namaste.

Made in the
USA
Lexington, KY

55410822R00157